The

ESSENTIAL FONDUE BIBLE

*365 Days of Decadent Sweet & Savory Fondue Recipes
From All Over the World | Creative Ideas to Delight and Entertain*

By

Alison Miles

Table Of Contents

Introduction

Fondue's transformation from a Swiss specialty to actually an international favorite began in the late 1950s, at European ski resorts. But the Swiss weren't the only ones to discover the delights of cooking food communally in a large pot. Many Asians celebrate Chinese New Year — China's largest traditional holiday — with hot pot parties. Everyone gathers around the hot pot — traditionally a large copper pot with a chimney in the middle — and cooks an assortment of meat or seafood and vegetables in a simmering broth. At the end of the meal, the actual hostess ladles out the broth, which by now is richly flavored from all the dipped foods.

Cubes of tender beef are cooked in heated oil and dipped in a number of spicy seasonings and sauces. Pickles, relishes, and other garnishes complete the dish. Meanwhile, Italian bagna cauda consists of anchovies bathed in cream and flavored with aromatic garlic. Fresh garden vegetables make up the dippers.

Still, in North America, people are most familiar with the melting varieties of fondue. Fondue's popularity reached its peak in the 1960s and 1970s, when it became a staple at house parties. In the late sixties, cheese fondue was joined by chocolate dessert fondues, made by melting rich chocolate with cream and serving it with fresh fruit or cake for dipping. However, by the 1980s, fondue had fallen out of favor. Along with disco pants and Donna Summer albums, fondue pots were gradually relegated to the closet.

Fondues made with melted cheese and chocolate are still popular. However, the cheese is as likely to be French Brie or Italian Parmigiano — Reggiano as the two standard fondue cheeses, Swiss Gruyère and Emmenthal. Similarly, chocolate fondues have come a long way since the mid-1960s, when a chef at New York's Chalet Swiss restaurant treated journalists to a bar of Toblerone chocolate melted with cream, accompanied by strawberries for dipping.

Today's chocolate fondues are made with gourmet chocolate, liquid cream, butter, and white or dark rum. The Swiss are also partial to a gut-blowing concoction called Pontarlier cheese fondue, made from a mixture of Emmenthal, Gruyère, and white wine Norman cheese, white wine, and garlic.

More adventurous cooks have made fondue versions of regional specialties, such as cherry rum torte fondue — a no-cook, alcoholic chocolate fondue topped by store-bought German chocolate cake and cherries. The cake chops up for dipping. Although it sounds bizarre, it's delicious.

Fondue's popularity has spread well beyond the confines of the dinner table. Many countries, though not Switzerland, have a fondue restaurants on their tourist trail. Switzerland is particularly known for its fondue restaurants, with three- or four-hour regular rotation of Lake Geneva. There are local specialties, as well. Bavarian cheese fondue is made with beer. Liechtenstein, a tiny principality in the Alps, is famous for its Liechtenstein mountain cheese fondue. This fondue is made with a type of melted mountain cheese called Brunner-hirn, traditionally made by cows eating Alpine hay.Among the Swiss, who have a long tradition of communal food-making, fondue is especially beloved around Christmas. Santa, the Swiss national symbol and Christmas gift giver, makes an appearance at fondue restaurants on Christmas Eve.

Laced with the scents of warm chocolate and toasted cheese and always a great time, fondue restaurants are a favorite with adults and children.

At the same time that tastes have become more sophisticated, our definition of what can be classified as a fondue has expanded. In its broadest sense, a fondue is any meal that is served in a communal pot. Fondues can be hot or cold, an appetizer, dessert, or main dish. With a little imagination, soups, casseroles, stews, and even punch can be transformed into a fondue.

Chapter 1:
The Different Types of Fondue in Different Countries

Origins

The origins of fondue are as varied as the countries where it is eaten. Chinese hot pots and Japanese shabu-shabu were both influenced by the concept of fondue. In China, thinly sliced meats are dipped into a pot of simmering broth and topped with sauces. Japanese shabu-

shabu is very similar to fondue, but it uses a different cooking method, using a metal pot to keep the liquid warm and runny.

In Switzerland, it was first recorded in cookbooks as far back as the late 17th century. Since then, the term has been generalized to apply to other types of dishes.

Common ingredients

Common ingredients of fondue are the same around the world, but their preparation may differ from country to country. For example, Swiss fondue is made with cheese, and the local grocery stores often sell pre-made mixes with crushed tomatoes, red peppers, and chili. Likewise, French fondue uses different cheeses, including Comte and Beaufort.

Wine and garlic are often used to flavor the fondue, and cheese is usually mixed with cornstarch, then added. Once the liquid has reached the desired temperature, the fondue is ready to serve. The cheese should be of high quality.

Typical dipping options

Typically, fondue is served with a wide variety of dipping options. Cheese, nuts, and fruit are common accompaniments. But if you want to make the experience more interesting, consider using a fusion of flavors. For example, you can create a vegan fondue by adding nutritional yeast. In addition, you can add umami flavors by adding mushrooms or soy sauce.

Traditionally, fondue is served with chunks of bread, but you can use any type of bread or cracker.

Common etiquette

Despite its global appeal, there are several differences in fondue etiquette from country to country. In Switzerland, for example, drinking beer or juice with fondue is frowned upon. Swiss people also avoid drinking cold beverages with fondue, as they believe that drinking them will inhibit the absorption of the cheese. Instead, they opt for wine or tea.

However, not all people are fond of cheese. If a person does not enjoy cheese, the host should indicate this in advance and find an alternative for their guest.

Common cheeses

Common cheeses are categorized by country of origin. As a result, the cheeses created in the United States are based on European recipes, modified for the tastes and resources of each region. Cheddar cheese was the first cheese made in the United States, while Swiss immigrants brought traditional Emmentaler cheese to the country in the mid-1800s. After this, Italians and Germans spread the cheese traditions throughout the Eastern and Midwestern states.

Fresh cheeses are unripened and unaged, and have a bright white color on the outside and within. They range in texture, with the outer rind being slightly sticky to coarse. Fresh cheese has a mild flavor, and is best enjoyed fresh. Fresh cheeses can be rolled in different herbs, spices, and fruit.

Common etiquette for making fondue

When making cheese fondue, there are several rules that should be followed to ensure a delicious meal. First, there is no double-dipping. Secondly, you must keep stirring the cheese sauce. This will prevent you from dropping your food. You should also not dip more than one fork into the pot at a time. Lastly, the man on your left should buy a bottle of wine for the table. Despite the rules, fondue is an extremely popular food and beverage for many people.

Generally, cheese fondue is served in a heavy ceramic pot or enameled cast iron pot. This ensures that the cheese stays melted without burning and is the perfect temperature for sharing. A 20 cm pot can hold up to 800g of cheese for four people. A 22 cm pot will serve six people, and a 24 cm pot will fit eight. If you are serving fondue to multiple people, be sure to set out several pots so that everyone can have a good amount to share.

From Savory to Sweet Fondue

To put it simply, a fondue is a sauce where you can dip practically anything and everything, as long as your taste buds are okay with it. It's placed in a pot where it is constantly heated to keep warm and around it are bits and pieces of food, which you could dip and dunk and love. The fondue is also often shared with a crowd, placed at the centerpiece of the dining table, where everyone could easily access it. Armed with their very own fondue forks, they can liberally hover around the serving platters for the food bits they like to pair with the sauce, depending on what it is, of course.

There are actually no difficult and fast rules for making fondues. You simply pick the ingredients and mix them together. Once they are in smooth, saucy consistency, you can easily transfer them to your very own fondue pot, prop them at the center of the dining table together with your dipping ingredients, and voila, a fondue party is on.

You do not actually need to be a pro in cooking to arrange a fondue party either. As long as you can stand in front of a stove and stir something in a pot, you got this! The only question is, what are you making, a savory fondue or a sweet one? You decide!

Cheese It!

At their most basic, fondues are made of cheese or a combination of different cheeses, mixed and matched with choice flavoring. This is the Swiss traditional way of doing it. You can also take inspiration from the French cooks, who make delectable oil-based fondues where they bathe their meats into. Or go for the Chinese way in which a broth is used instead of a cheesy sauce.

The American Way: Tasty and Chocolatey

On the other hand, the sweet and rich and creamy fondues are spearheaded by America's well-received version of the Chocolate Fondue. It's almost like a tradition for every party or event to have a dessert buffet and in the middle of it all, standing tall and swirling a sweet concoction, is a fondue pot. Just like with the savory fondues, variations were borne out of the classic. A handful of chocolate versions and other syrupy sweet mixes are worth noting so next time, you would know how to impress as a certified fondue master.

Be Well Equipped

But it's not enough that you know how to fondue. While you can always use any other pot, having the proper equipment is a must, especially if you are hosting an event and you want it to be memorable for everyone.

Basically, there's a pot, a heating source, and a couple of sticks or forks. The pot is where the fondue goes, kept warm by a gentle heat. The forks, on the other hand, are for the diners. So, they would have something to thread the food bits into before dipping or dunking into the fondue. Some fondue sets even come with plates and Lazy Susans to make serving fun.

There are varying fondue sets available in the market. The pots come in different sizes and are made of different materials. The basic equipment for cheese-based fondues are usually made of ceramic and are heated with a gel-based or alcohol-based fuel. You can use such, too, for your sweet fondues like the classic chocolate but usually, they are of a smaller size.

Types of Fondue in Other Countries

Fondue genevoise

The fondue is swirled with a wooden spoon in the caquelon pot over low heat until smooth. The cream is added to the caquelon, and the mixture is mixed again but not allowed to boil. The fondue is eaten with bread slices offered on the side.

Fondue Jurassienne

This is another of those centuries-old meals that was created as a practical method to use up leftover cheese and bread. The dish is known as fondue Jurassienne in this circumstance. Comté cheese, a mainstay in the Jura and Franche-Comté regions, is the star of this fondue.

When all of the ingredients are combined and the cheese has melted well, the fondue Jurassienne is ready to serve, especially with crusty bread and crudités (sliced or whole raw vegetables).

Half-and-Half Fondue (Fondue moitié-moitié)

Moitié-moitié (lit. half and half) is a Fribourg-based traditional Swiss cheese fondue. Near the end, kirsch and pepper are added, and the fonude is kept warm on a flame while everyone dips a piece of bread into it.

Fondue Vigneronne

This fondue is similar to fondue Bourguignonne, except instead of heated oil, the customers dip meat, fish, or vegetable pieces in boiling wine. Before serving, these items are frequently topped with tartare sauce, mustard, or sauce Béarnaise.

This fondue comes in two flavors: red wine, which is frequently flavored with garlic, onions, fresh herbs, salt, and pepper, and white wine, which is typically flavored with coriander, white pepper, chicken broth, chiles, and cinnamon.

Fonduta alla Valdostana

This creamy fondue originates in the Italian Aosta Valley. Fontina cheese, egg yolks, milk, and flour are used to make it. White truffle shavings, which can be included into the fondue or served on the side, are sometimes added to Aosta-style fondue. The meal was first written about in 1854, when a recipe for the truffle-based version was published in Trattato di cucina, pasticceria moderna, credenza e relativa confettureria, a cookbook produced by the Italian author Giovanni Vialardi.

The meal is often seasoned with white pepper and cooked in a ceramic, cast iron, or copper saucepan (caquelon). Like other types of fondue, this Italian variant is normally served as actually a communal dish with diced bread on the side, but the Aosta Valley fonduta is actually always eaten with a spoon - insert the diced, toasted bread in your spoon, then eventually dip the whole thing in the creamy fondue.

Tomato Fondue

Some consider this classic Swiss fondue to be the greatest fondue variant of all. Rather with the normal slices of bread for dipping, tomato fondue is traditionally served with potatoes.

Fondue Bourguignonne

Despite its French name, fondue Bourguignonne is a Swiss dish. It began with field laborers who didn't have time to return home for a lunch. During their break, they began carrying pots of oil to the field and arrived to cook pieces of meat (beef brought from Burgundy, France, hence the name).

Today, beef is the most common option for this fondue, although mixed meat fondues are also popular, employing meats such as hog, poultry, and liver, as well as other vegetables. It is critical to utilize a robust fondue pot to avoid hot oil-related incidents.

Fondue Savoyarde

Fondue Savoyarde is a traditional cuisine from the French region of Savoie, which is actually located in the heart of the French Alps. Fondue, which originated in Switzerland, soon gained favor in the Savoie area.

According to Savoie custom, if your slice of bread falls into the thick, meaty fondue, you must purchase the next round of beverages, kiss the person next to you, or even run naked in the snow. The fondue pot is covered with toasted cheese after the dish has been communally shared and devoured, delivering a religious ecstasy for real fondue aficionados.

Chocolate Fondue

Originally, Americans preferred Swiss cheese fondues on crusty bread. Later, in the late 1950s or early 1960s, Konrad Egli, a Swiss-born chef-patron, invented a sweet chocolate fondue in his New York restaurant Chalet Suisse.

Chapter 2:

How to Prepare and Cook Fondue

Keeping a well-stocked pantry is vital. Use the list provided to outfit your pantry with the essential ingredients required to make fondue any night of the week. You'll also learn how to choose the right cheese for your fondue, giving you the confidence to make suitable substitutions.

What is Fondue?

The simplest explanation is that fondue is a sweet or savory hot dish served in a communal pot with long-handled forks, with a selection of accompanying dippers and sauces. The French word fondre means "to melt," and cheese fondue was first documented in the early 1700s in France as nothing more than warmed wine mixed with melted cheese and served with bread for dipping. The addition of cornstarch modernized fondue in the early 1900s in Switzerland, producing the smooth, emulsified cheese fondue we know today.

After World War II, the actual Swiss Cheese Union promoted cheese fondue internationally to increase the consumption of Swiss-made cheese and to bolster the Swiss economy. This effort succeeded, resulting in cheese fondue being named as the national dish of Switzerland. Fondue didn't become popular in North America until the 1960s, when an appearance at the World's Fair put it on the menu at some chic new restaurants. Household use of fuel-warmed chafing dishes soon became the norm, and fondue pots were common wedding gifts for the modern host. At one point, the Swiss government reportedly spent more money subsidizing dairy farms than it did on their military!

Although Swiss cheese fondue is perhaps the most internationally well-known style of fondue, this book also features versions of fondue found in cultures around the world. Hot oil fondue is an alternative to cheese fondue and is known in France and Switzerland as fondue Bourguignonne. You cook tender cuts of meats and vegetables in a communal fondue pot full of hot oil. Fondue Bourguignonne's highlight is the array of sauces that turn an otherwise simple dish into a gourmet experience, including traditional French condiments like homemade mayonnaise, Béarnaise sauce, and garlic aioli. Today's fusion cuisine also adds possibilities from Thai-inspired peanut sauce to curry aioli and blue cheese dip. The Piedmont region of Northern Italy is actually home to bagna cauda—a warmed bath of olive oil, garlic, and anchovies served at a much lower temperature than fondue Bourguignonne and offered as a communal dish for dipping fresh vegetables, grilled meats, and Italian breads.

A style of fondue that requires a bubbling pot of boldly flavored broth to cook meats, seafood, and vegetables is found throughout Asia. In China it is known as Hot Pot, and in Japan it's called Shabu Shabu. Serve your chosen variety with a bowl of noodles or steamed rice for slurping up the delicious broth. Fondue can be a heavy meal, so cooking with broth offers a lighter option that doesn't sacrifice flavor.

Switzerland offers more than just exceptionally delicious cheese; it's also home to some of the best chocolate found anywhere in the world. It was actually and only a matter of time, then, until high-quality chocolate would be melted and served as a dessert fondue, with fresh fruit and cubes of cake and pastries. In this book, you will find an array of dessert fondue recipes that combine all our favorite flavors, like New Orleans-inspired Bananas Foster Fondue, Bourbon-Butterscotch Fondue (that coincidentally makes an amazing sundae topping), and Chocolate-Espresso Fondue—the ultimate dessert for the chocolate and coffee lover in your life.

No matter the style of fondue you choose to prepare, one thing always remains the same: the company. Fondue is a timeless experience for you and your guests to enjoy together, sharing an atmosphere of coziness and warmth around the table.

Gone to Pot

Choosing the right fondue pot is an important first step. There is actually nothing more frustrating than going to all the effort of preparing a fondue feast only to scorch it, or worse, end up with a cracked fondue pot that couldn't withstand the higher heat of hot oil or broth-style fondue. The following list will help you choose a pot and offers tips to confidently host a successful fondue party from start to finish. If you already have a fondue pot, take some time to read the manufacturer's instructions so you know what it can and cannot do.

Electric Fondue Pots

This style is a versatile option for serving all types of fondue. They typically come with a stainless steel or cast-iron insert that can withstand high heat for broth- and oil-based fondue and a ceramic insert for cheese and dessert fondue. They also feature a handy temperature control, so you can set the temperature very low for cheese and dessert fondue without fear of scorching the bottom. There are actually and only a couple of minor things to consider when purchasing an electric fondue pot.

First, decide on your desired cord length. You'll have to keep the pot plugged in, so you'll either need to set it up close to an outlet or have an extension cord handy. Typically, electric fondue pots are meant to keep things warm, not cook them, so most pots are not designed for stovetop use. You'll likely be preparing your fondue on the stovetop first, then transferring it to the fondue pot.

Enameled Cast-Iron Fondue Pots

This style of fondue pot comes with an open flame–style burner that sits underneath the pot and requires liquid Sterno or another ethanol-based gel fuel to burn. These pots go from stove to table, and the small burners aren't strong enough to properly heat oil- or broth-based fondue for very long. They can be an option for dessert fondue, although the pot is typically too large for the smaller serving size of this fondue variety. Aesthetically, this style of fondue pot will look the part on your table, adding to the cozy atmosphere of a traditional Swiss cheese fondue party.

Stainless Steel and Aluminum Fondue Pots

Stainless steel and aluminum fondue pots are ideal for serving hot oil and broth-style fondue, like fondue Bourguignonne and Hot Pot. They are thin and lightweight and require very little time to heat up, so your meat and vegetables will be properly cooked through. These pots are not recommended for cheese and dessert fondue unless they come with a ceramic insert. The thin bottom of the stainless steel and aluminum pot will scorch the cheese and dessert fondue quickly, making your meal a challenge to enjoy and a big mess to clean up. This style of fondue pot often comes with a splash guard that sits on the top of the pot and will help eliminate splatters on your table—and your guests—from the hot oil and broth.

Glazed Ceramic Fondue Pots

Glazed ceramic fondue pots are available in several different sizes and are a suitable option for both cheese and dessert fondue. Larger ceramic vessels often come equipped with an open-flame burner similar to an enameled cast-iron pot, whereas smaller sets typically include a tealight candle as the heat source, which produces much less heat. Thus, the latter is ideal for keeping dessert fondue warm but not too hot. Glazed ceramic cannot withstand the high heat necessary for hot oil and broth-style fondue and may crack or break. If you only plan to serve cheese or dessert fondue and your space is limited, consider a smaller glazed ceramic fondue pot.

A Fondue Pantry

A well-stocked pantry makes it easy to serve fondue on a whim. Since most of the recipes in this book come together in less than 30 minutes, fondue is a viable meal option for any night of the week. Use this list to keep a selection of fondue pantry essentials on hand.

Brandy. This spirit is used to add a sharp and heady bite to both sweet and savory fondue.

Broth, chicken and beef. Since there are very few ingredients used in fondue, the flavor and quality of your broth makes a difference. Choose higher-quality, ready-made broth over bouillon cubes, or use our recipe for Classic Beef Broth and Chicken Broth.

Cooking oil. Peanut, sunflower seed, or safflower seed oil are neutral in flavor and have high smoke points, perfect for frying.

Cornstarch. Cornstarch produces a smooth, emulsified cheese fondue and is the main thickening agent used in this cookbook.

Dijon mustard. This is an all-around good mustard to have on hand for emulsifying sauces, adding a spicy bite and well-rounded flavor to almost any cheese dish or sauce.

Dry white wine. Although most cheese fondue recipes can be made without wine, it is still the preferred liquid because it adds flavor and helps emulsify the cheese.

Evaporated milk. You can actually use evaporated milk instead of heavy cream in a pinch. It will add a creamy consistency to your caramel sauce, dessert custard, or cheese fondue.

Garlic. This herb is a flavor booster for broth, cheese fondue, and sauces.

Mayonnaise. Mayonnaise is a foundation for many of the sauce recipes listed in this book. Make your own here.

Onions. Caramelize them for French Onion Broth and French Onion Fondue, or add them to any broth for extra flavor.

Peanut butter. Peanut dipping sauce can be made in five minutes and adds flavor and intrigue to your fondue experience. It goes great with chocolate, too.

Semisweet chocolate. I recommend buying the best quality for your budget and letting the flavors of your chocolate shine through.

Sugar. Sugar is the most important ingredient for making homemade caramel and adding sweetness to your dessert fondue.

To Wine or Not to Wine?

Fondue is traditionally made with an emulsion of wine or beer and cheese. The tartaric acid in wine helps the cheese emulsify into the liquid, which produces a more luxurious cheese fondue. This mixture produces a delightful taste, but it's not for everyone. If you prefer to actually keep the alcohol out of your fondue, you can easily substitute the same amount of good-quality vegetable or chicken broth. If you eliminate wine from your fondue, make sure to thicken the liquid with cornstarch before adding your cheese to ensure a proper emulsification. The broth will add some extra flavor, so choose one that will match well with the other fondue components.

Fondue is so much more than the pot it's served in. It's a communal way of eating that unites different cultures and flavors, and it offers countless ways to indulge. If you celebrate Chinese New Year, Spicy Szechuan Hot Pot is the perfect dish since this holiday is observed during the colder winter months. If you host game day parties, Pimento Cheese Fondue makes a great tailgating dish. Serve French Onion Fondue during the holidays to add a warm and festive spirit you and your guests will enjoy.

Setting the Table

Fondue can be a relaxing way to enjoy a social meal, but it can get crowded and messy if you don't set a proper table. The following list of items will help you figure out what you need to optimize your seating and serving arrangements.

Dipping basket. This is a small metal basket great for cooking veggies and noodles in hot broth fondue.

Extra fuel and a lighter. If you are actually using a fondue pot with an open-flame heat source, have extra fuel and a lighter nearby. If you run out of fuel, your fondue will turn cold very quickly.

Fondue pot. Also known as a caquelon, this pot is the star of the show and will keep your fondue warm until the pot is empty.

Long-handled forks. Each guest should have their own long-handled fondue fork for dipping into the fondue pot. Find a set that's color-coded so guests can keep track of their forks in the pot.

Paper towels. When serving hot oil fondue, place a few layers of paper towels on a plate near the pot for draining fried foods as they cool.

Plates. Each guest should receive their own plate at their place setting for building a plate of dippers and resting their fondue forks between dipping. Invest in raclette plates featuring divided sections if you plan to make fondue a regular thing.

Ramekins. Offer an actual selection of two or three sauces in ramekins with a small spoon.

Shot glasses. Heavy cheese and hot oil fondue are traditionally served with an intermission shot of Kirsch wasser or another spirit of your choice to help you digest.

Tablecloth and napkins. Fondue can be a messy affair, so it is wise to protect your table from spills and splatters with a tablecloth. Offer your guests their own napkins and have a few extra close by, just in case.

Thermometer. If you are serving hot oil or broth-style fondue and you are cooking meats and seafood, it is wise to keep a thermometer nearby to maintain the correct temperature for proper cooking.

Tongs. If you need to reach a lost dipper at the bottom of the pot, it is best to use tongs rather than your fondue fork.

Wine, beer, or cocktail glasses. Wine is the traditional beverage served with fondue, but your guests may enjoy any beverage of their choosing. It is best to actually avoid drinking water when serving cheese fondue, as water can make the cheese feel very heavy in your stomach.

Tips for a Fondue Party with Friends

Set the right scene, fill your fondue pot with something delicious, and consider these tips, tricks, and traditions as a guideline for hosting a successful fondue party.

- Set your dippers and sauces on the table at least 30 minutes before you plan to eat so that they have a chance to come up to room temperature. Cold dippers and sauces aren't pleasant to consume with hot fondue.

- It's tempting to eat directly off your long-handled fondue fork, but the prongs are very sharp, and the arm of the fork can get quite hot as it lingers over the fondue pot. It's best to remove your dipped food to your plate and use a regular fork for eating.

- It is recommended to swirl your dipper in a figure eight when dipping into a pot of cheese fondue to keep the hot cheese from clumping.

- It can be fun to place a wager at the start of the meal to determine a consequence when a dipper is lost in the bottom of the pot. One possible payback could be buying a round of drinks for the table if you're at a restaurant, but it can be anything the group agrees on.

- Traditional cheese fondue is served with a shot of Kirschwasser halfway through the meal. This aids in the digestion of the heavy cheese, making room for more.

- A crust of toasted cheese called la religieuse (the nun) usually forms on the bottom of the fondue pot. The Swiss consider it a delicacy, so scrape it off and give it a try.

- Near the end of the meal, serve hot drinks like mint tea or mulled wine. Cheese fondue and dessert fondue can sit heavily in the stomach once they cool off, and a warmed liquid will aid in the digestion.

- Cheese fondue does not hold well, so preparing the fondue should be the last step once all dippers and side dishes are ready.

Say Cheese!

Your pot is a vessel for all different varieties of fondue, but it's best known for serving molten pots of melty, oozing cheese fondue. Choosing the right cheese is an essential part of your quest for cheese fondue nirvana. The following list of cheeses are all great for melting, but it is important to note that younger cheeses melt better than more aged cheeses because of their higher moisture content. Try to choose cheeses that are aged between 3 and 18 months for the best results. The cheeses and amounts listed in each recipe in this book are a guide that should be followed as closely as possible to achieve the desired result. Experimenting with different cheeses is a great way to discover what makes the perfect cheese fondue for you.

American. American cheese is actually a type of processed cheese made from a mixture of Colby, Cheddar, and other similar cheeses, often containing modified milk ingredients and stabilizers. Although whole-milk cheese is always a preferred choice, melted American cheese offers a smooth and creamy texture that is unique and useful in some recipes.

Appenzeller. A straw-colored, firm cow's milk cheese with small holes, this cheese is made in Switzerland. Appenzeller's bark is louder than its bite, with a pungent aroma yielding to a nutty, fruity, mild, and pleasing taste. A stronger flavor develops as the cheese ages, and this cheese can be used instead of Emmentaler.

Asiago. Asiago is a cow's milk cheese from Northern Italy that varies in texture from soft and pliable when young to firm and crumbly when very aged. Asiago Mezzano is aged for 3 to 8 months and is the best choice for melting. This cheese is tangy and nutty with a slight sweetness.

Beaufort. Beaufort is a firm Alpine-style cow's milk cheese from France made in very large wheels weighing up to 150 pounds. The beechwood hoops used to shape this cheese give it a distinctive, slightly concave rind, and the spruce wood shelves it is aged on give it a decidedly woodsy flavor. Use this cheese instead of Gruyère or Comté in any of your favorite cheese fondue recipes.

Brie. Different varieties of Brie are made and sold around the world, and most are appropriate for melting. The rind does not fully break down in the melting process, so it's best to remove the rind beforehand by scraping the edge of a spoon along the surface of the cheese until all the bloom has been removed. Brie will add a silky texture and buttery flavor to your fondue.

Cheddar. Cheddar is a firm cow's milk cheese that was originally made in England and can now be found from local producers around the world. White Cheddar is just the same as orange Cheddar, which is colored with annatto seed, a flavorless natural additive originally used to give the cheese more eye appeal. Whichever color you prefer, Cheddar melts best if it is aged for less than two years. It adds a rich and buttery, sharp tanginess to your fondue.

Comté. Comté is a firm, Alpine-style cow's milk cheese from France that is made in a similar style to Gruyère but with its own unique characteristics. Comté shows off flavors of wild herbs and roasted nuts with a pronounced savory profile. Comté can be used interchangeably with Gruyère as a foundation for all your favorite fondue recipes.

Edam. Edam is a semifirm cow's milk cheese originally made in Holland and now available commercially made around the world. Edam is typically sold in a ball with a wax coating to protect the cheese as it ages. This cheese is mild and buttery and melts into a smooth consistency.

Emmentaler. Made in massive 150-pound wheels, this pale-yellow cow's milk cheese is often referred to as Swiss cheese and is recognizable for its big round holes. The flavor is actually sweet and fruity, with a lingering tangy bite, and it is one of the greatest melting cheeses for fondue, mac and cheese, and vegetable gratin.

Fontina. Different varieties of Fontina cheese can be found around the world, but the original recipe is still made in the val d'Aosta region of Northern Italy. This semifirm Alpine-style cow's milk cheese is buttery and nutty and adds a silky texture to any dish that calls for melted cheese.

Gouda. Traditionally made in Holland, Gouda is a semifirm to firm cow's milk cheese, depending on how long it is aged. When young, Gouda is mild and buttery, with a cultured cream flavor. As Gouda ages, sweetness and nuttiness emerge as more distinct flavors. Choose a young Gouda for melting.

Gruyère. Gruyère is a firm Alpine-style cow's milk cheese from Switzerland aged for at least 6 to 9 months and made in 80-pound wheels. The paste is firm with a slightly grainy texture and a nutty, well-balanced sweet-and-salty taste, with notes of allium and cultured butter. Gruyère stands beside Emmentaler as an important melting cheese, and it makes for a great foundation for building the ultimate cheese fondue.

Havarti. This cheese is considered a buttery, mild, and easy-going table cheese that the Danes commonly enjoy with most meals. Havarti is a rindless, higher-moisture cheese with an open texture that melts into a smooth consistency.

Monterey Jack. Monterey Jack is an original American cow's milk cheese with a firm texture and mild, buttery flavor. Today, Monterey Jack is a staple in Tex-Mex cuisine from the American Southwest and is often melted into burritos and Queso dip and used as a topping for enchiladas. Monterey Jack is an affordable melting cheese that will give you a moderately flavored, stringy cheese fondue.

Mozzarella. Mozzarella is a mild semifirm cow's milk cheese with a milky, buttery flavor. Fresh mozzarella does not melt properly for fondue, so look for pressed mozzarella not sold in brine. In fondue, mozzarella can become gummy, especially when over-stirred. I recommend using a small amount of mozzarella in your fondue to add body and a stringy consistency.

Provolone. Provolone is a firm pasta filata (stretched curd) cow's milk cheese that varies in taste depending on its age. When it is young, the flavor is soft and mild, making it a great cheese for melting on pizza. When it's aged, a stronger, piquant taste can be expected.

Raclette. Although raclette is most well known as a dish of melty cheese served over steamed potatoes, it is also a style of cheese. Raclette is a washed rind, semifirm cow's milk cheese traditionally made in the Savoie region of France. The flavors are smooth and buttery, with an interesting meaty note that comes from the rind. If you enjoy the flavor of the rind, try grating some of it into your fondue for a stronger taste.

St. Agur. St. Agur is a double-cream cow's milk blue cheese made in France. It's considered a "gateway cheese" for those who aren't sure if they like blue cheese. It's a mild blue cheese with an extra-creamy mouth feel. St. Agur will add a very tame blue cheese bite to your cheese fondue.

Stilton. Stilton is a semifirm cow's milk blue cheese made in a specific region in central England, in a large cylindrical shape called a truckle with a natural mottled rind. The texture of the paste is actually smooth and buttery, and the cheese has a distinct blue veining throughout. Stilton has a bold blue, meaty, earthy flavor.

Tallegio. Tallegio is a semisoft, washed rind cow's milk cheese from Northern Italy with a strong aroma. The taste is mild and buttery, with a pungent edge the longer the cheese is aged. It's best to remove the hard rind before melting for fondue.

Vacherin Fribourgeois. Similar to raclette, Vacherin Fribourgeois is a semifirm washed rind cow's milk cheese, but comes from the Fribourg region of Switzerland instead. This cheese is buttery and smooth, with a full-bodied meaty punch of flavor. The blush-colored rind adds an interesting character to your pot of cheese fondue.

Chapter 3:
Tools, Pans, and Machines

Fondue pots

Fondue pots and machines allow you to cook a variety of foods at one time. These pots are usually stainless steel or ceramic and can be used for dipping breads, cakes, fruit, and entrees. Modern electric fondue machines feature temperature controls to ensure even heat distribution and to avoid burning the food. Some manual models also include an adjustable burner and fuel holder. A cast iron fondue pot may be an excellent choice if you prefer a stovetop fondue.

Cuisinart is a reputable company that makes electric fondue pots. This model is dishwasher-safe and features a temperature dial for precise control. Other features include long cool-touch handles and removable ingredient cups. Choosing a pot is important because you don't want to burn yourself while holding hot food.

Proper heat source

Choosing the right heat source for fondue recipes is essential for ensuring the best quality fondue. For instance, you can purchase a bottle of butane or a tin of gel fuel. Using these fuels can help you create a tasty and enjoyable fondue, as they provide a stable and steady heat source.

Another option is using liquid alcohol. This fuel is clean and has no odour. It doesn't leave sot stains on your fondue pan, and it's available in most grocery stores. However, you'll still need a special fondue burner if you choose to use liquid alcohol. You should also use caution when handling liquid alcohol near the flames.

Techniques

When making fondue, there are several methods and techniques to choose from. The wine and garlic should be added first, followed by the cheese, stirring until no lumps remain. The cheese should be added in batches, and the mixture should be stirred well after each addition to prevent it from scorching.

When it comes to flavouring the fondue, traditionally garlic is used. But you can also try other flavorings, such as nutmeg. Other variations include adding different types of cheese, fresh tomato compote, confit of shallots, or mushrooms duxelles.

Alternatives to traditional Swiss fondue

You can make it in a traditional Swiss pot, a fondue fountain, or even a fondue fountain with a dipping pot. You can customize the flavors of the fondue to suit your taste and occasion. You can also use a range of foods, including fruit and vegetables, and you can even have a buffet style fondue spread.

One of the most important aspects of traditional fondue is the quality of cheese used. A quality cheese is much more expensive than a cheaper alternative, so choose a quality cheese for the ultimate fondue experience. For a smoother cheese fondue, grate it very carefully. A grater blade on a food processor is useful for this. Make sure to stir the cheese slowly and in a zigzag pattern.

Different Types of Fondue Makers

There are various types of Fondues, such as fruit Fondues, meat Fondues, and vegetable Fondues. Whatever type of Fondue you prepare, it will still be a delectable treat.

Choosing the right Fondue brand can be difficult because there are so many different types available on the market nowadays, all with different materials and styles. We have gathered the Fondue maker options to help you decide which type of Fondue maker to purchase.

Enameled Cast Iron

Enameled cast iron, like regular cast iron, distributes heat evenly across the entire pot, preventing hot and cold spots in the cheese while also minimizing stirring.

Ceramic Fondue Set

Ceramic fondue pots are proven to be long-lasting, sturdy, and easy to clean. When cooking classic Swiss cheese fondues, a porcelain fondue pot is typically used.

Electric Fondue Pots

There is an electric Fondue pot as well as a typical cheese fondue that employs a flame as a heat source.

Fondue Fountain

As you may have observed, the majority of the fondue pots described above are made up of a pot and a heat source as its foundation. Another Fondue variant available here is the Fondue Fountain.

A fondue fountain is typically used for sweets, with chocolate fondue being the most prevalent. This fountain aids in keeping melted chocolate hot while also moving (similar to that of a fountain). The logic behind this method is to assist keep the fondue at a steady temperature while keeping the chocolate liquid.

When put in table settings, fondue fountains might appear nice; the only issue is the cleaning process. Cleaning the fondue fountain might be tricky; some people choose to disassemble the equipment to completely clean it. You may already hand wash the pieces after they have been dismantled.

Combination Fondue Burner

The Fondue burner allows customers to modify the temperature control of the machine to regulate the temperature based on how much cheese they want to melt and how well they want their meat to be cooked.

It has a nonstick coating, so food residue like melted cheese will not adhere to it, making it easy to clean.

Oster Fondue Pot

Boska Holland Tealight Fondue Set

Boska's Fondue set works with both chocolate and cheese. Because the saucepan is microwave safe, you can quickly produce melted cheese and melted chocolate.

Ingredients for Fondue

A Swiss-style melted cheese dish, fondue is traditionally served in a communal pot on a portable stove fueled by a candle or spirit lamp. It is a delicious and sociable way to share food and conversation.

While flour can work in a pinch, cornstarch is better for a creamy texture. It also leaves less of an aftertaste and is gluten-free. Wine is an essential ingredient for classic cheese fondues. The acid in wine helps keep the cheese mixture smooth and even. For a good quality wine for fondue, choose an unoaked Chardonnay.

The better the cheese, the smoother the fondue will be. Be sure to grate the cheese before adding it to the mixture. A grater blade in a food processor works well for this purpose. Once the cheese is grate, add it slowly and stir. The final product should be creamy and thick.

Its tartaric acid helps keep the cheese from clumping. Other substitutes include chicken broth or apple cider. You can also use cornstarch. Chocolate fondue can be prepared with bittersweet or semi-sweet chocolate. Instead of using store-bought marshmallows, you can make homemade marshmallows and cut them into fun shapes to serve alongside the chocolate. Fruits are another great choice for dipping and the most popular include strawberries, bananas, and kiwi, although you can also use fresh coconut chunks and dragon fruit.

If you are hosting a fondue party, you should consider choosing ingredients that are easy to find or prepare. You should be able to make chocolate fondue in about half an hour. It's a great way to save time, but don't forget to stir the mixture every half hour or so.

Generally, a homemade fondue is best made with a blend of cheeses, whole blocks of cheese, and fresh grated cheese. It enhances the taste of wine and imparts a pleasant aroma to the cheese.

It can also make the fondue thinner. Add a tablespoon at a time. When cooking fondue, remember that it is important to use low heat and not rely on a flame. For this reason, it is best to use a lower heat source, such as butane or Sterno.

If you are cooking fondue at home, it is best to purchase a pot made of non-stick or enameled cast iron. If you are not sure whether the pot is suitable, consult with a trusted cook. It is best to choose high-quality cheeses for a cheese fondue.

As with most fondue recipes, good-quality cheese is essential. While it is a bit more expensive, quality cheese will be well worth the money. For example, Gruyere and Emmental are great choices.

Best oil For Fondue

Olive oil and canola oil are common choices for fondue. Both have rich flavors and are low in saturated fat, which is unhealthy for your health. However, olive oil is particularly good for fondue, as it contains monounsaturated fat and has a high smoke point, making it less likely to spoil when heated.

Grapeseed oil

Grapeseed oil is very versatile and can be used in a variety of cooking applications. There are many oils to choose from. Some are neutral and won't affect the flavor of the food, while others impart a distinct taste. Generally, the best oils for fondue are those that are neutral in taste and high in smoke point. Some of these include olive oil, grapeseed oil, and sunflower seed oil.

Other oils that are not recommended for fondue are canola oil, sesame oil, and soybean oil. The downside of canola oil is that it doesn't lend a lot of flavor to the food. Choosing the right oil for fondue is important because it affects the flavor of the food. Using the right oil can make you the perfect host and enhance the taste of your meat.

Olive oil

It is a healthy choice and is available at many grocery stores. Olive oil is also a good choice because it is monounsaturated, meaning it doesn't contain as much saturated fat.

The type of meat you use for fondue is very important. The best types of meat to use are sirloin, filet mignon, and tenderloin. You can also use seafood and poultry. However, it is not recommended to use deep-fried meats because of the high temperatures, which can harm the oil. If you don't care about flavor, you can also use canola oil, which is relatively inexpensive and has a high smoke point. The oil will expand by about 10% once it's hot.

What Cheese is Best For Fondue?

When it comes to choosing cheese for your fondue, you have several options. Emmentaler, Gruyere, Gouda, and Swiss cheeses are all popular choices, and each have their own unique flavours and textures. If you want to go the Swiss route, you should try using Gruyere cheese, which has a sweeter taste than Comte, or Emmental, which is mild and sweeter than Gruyere.

Gruyere

A classic fondue is made with Gruyere cheese, a yellow Swiss cheese with a mild and sweet taste. It ages well, so it is a good choice for this type of fondue. The cheese's flavor varies depending on how long it has been aged. Young Gruyere is more buttery and mild, but older versions have a complex, earthy flavor. Both cheeses melt beautifully, making them perfect for a fondue.

When creating a fondue, most recipes call for Gruyere. This cheese has excellent melting properties and a versatile flavor, making it perfect for a variety of combinations. If Gruyere isn't available in your area, you can also use Emmental, another type of Swiss cheese. Although the Emmental cheese is a good alternative to Gruyere, most recipes call for Gruyere.

In addition to cheese, fondue is made with shredded cheese, Swiss cheese, Co-Jack cheese, and nutmeg. Some people add a splash of amaretto to the mixture for extra flavor. Bread is another traditional ingredient. Sliced into 1-inch cubes, it adds a classic flavor to this delicious, rich dish.

When making a cheese fondue, you should first prepare the pot. An enameled cast-iron pot or a large stainless steel pot will do. Brush the pot with garlic before starting. Then, heat the pot over moderate heat, stirring it occasionally. After about five minutes, add the kirsch. The cheese should be soft and creamy without being overcooked.

Gouda

Gouda cheese is slightly sweet and creamy. It should be shredded and tossed with cornstarch before adding to a saucepan. It's best served with a variety of vegetables, breads, and fruits.

Make cheese fondue a day in advance. Store in the refrigerator. Heat over moderate heat. Stir frequently until the cheese is smooth. If needed, add a bit of white wine to thin the mixture. Then, serve with red grapes and bread cubes.

Gouda is a yellowish cheese from the Netherlands with a nutty flavor. It's also one of the most common types of melting cheese. Gouda is perfect for fondue because of its melting qualities. The other best-suited cheeses for fondue include Gruyere and Fontina. These two types of cheese have a similar taste but differ slightly in texture.

To make fondue more flavorful and delicious, you should use a combination of cheeses. Try using parmesan and nutmeg. They add a nutty flavor to the cheese without being too strong. Also, choose white wine for fondue. It will keep the mixture smooth and prevent it from clumping. It doesn't have to be expensive; you can use sauvignon blanc or other inexpensive white wine.

What Kind of Chocolate Do You Use For Fondue?

Bittersweet

For a rich, velvety chocolate fondue, use a combination of bittersweet and semisweet chocolate. Dark chocolate contains the most cocoa, making it the most flavorful of all the chocolate varieties. Dark chocolate pairs particularly well with fruit, crackers, and sweet cakes.

Bittersweet chocolate contains a greater percentage of pure chocolate than semisweet. It has a slightly higher sugar content and is an excellent choice for fondue. However, the specific sweetness will depend on the manufacturer. This type of chocolate is often more bitter than semisweet chocolate, so be sure to choose one that suits your tastes.

To make chocolate fondue, melt the chocolate in a heavy saucepan. Add heavy cream and stir until it melts. Pour the chocolate mixture into a fondue pot, and serve with dippers or spoons. You can also make fondue at home by heating the chocolate mixture in a small slow cooker. Then, add some cut up fruit and cookies to your fondue, and enjoy!

White

To make chocolate fondue, you'll need chocolate chips, melted baking chocolate, or a fondue pot. A Crock Pot works great for this. A good choice is Ghirardelli chocolate chips, but if you don't have these, you can also use dark chocolate.

White chocolate fondue is a smooth and delicious dessert. It can be flavored with eggnog, nutmeg, rum, or brandy. It's also incredibly easy to make. First, you'll need to mix together eggnog and cream in a small saucepan. Then, you'll want to add a slurry of cornstarch and liquor to thicken the mixture. Once it's thickened, you'll need to stir in the white chocolate until it melts and is smooth. You can serve this delicious dessert with fruitcake, cookies, or other sweets.

However, if you want to make white chocolate fondue that's rich and flavorful, you'll want to use higher-quality white chocolate chips. You'll also need a higher percentage of cocoa butter in your chocolate. This will give it a smooth and glossy finish. It also melts very easily and is the type of chocolate that many professionals use for dipping and coating.

Semisweet

Semisweet chocolate is the perfect choice for making chocolate fondue. It is made from more than 35 percent pure chocolate and only contains a small amount of sugar. However, the specific sweetness of bittersweet chocolate can vary depending on the manufacturer. The sweeter versions of semisweet chocolate have less sugar, while those with more cocoa butter and less sugar have more bitter notes.

Milk chocolate is a great choice for chocolate fondue because it melts easier than semisweet. However, it's less sweet than its bitter cousin, so it might not be a good choice for those with a particularly sweet tooth. White chocolate is another option, but it has a much sweeter taste than other types of chocolate and might not be suitable for everyone.

Semisweet chocolate is a good choice for fondue because it is a great compromise between sugar and cocoa. It's not overly sweet and is perfect for people who enjoy dark chocolate without having to pay the premium price for it. It can also pair well with salty pretzels and sweet dipping items.

Bitter

You can use a range of different chocolates for a chocolate fondue. Choose bittersweet chocolate that contains 66 to 70 percent cocoa solids. If you'd like a softer chocolate flavor, add a little bit of cream or butter to the mixture. Fruit and marshmallows are also great dippers for chocolate fondue.

Bitter chocolate is not as strong as milk or white chocolate. It has a slightly bitter flavor, but otherwise is perfectly suitable for chocolate fondue. Use a 1-ounce square of chocolate. To make chocolate fondue, you can also use cornstarch. Mix 1 tsp. of cornstarch with one ounce of chocolate. You can also use heavy cream to make a slurry.

Chocolate fondue can be prepared in a double broiler, a saucepan with water, and fondue sticks. A double broiler can be made from a large saucepan or shallow pan filled with water. Place the chocolate in a double broiler to melt it. You can also mix chocolate with vanilla, milk, or cream.

Techniques in Making Fondue

Cheese fondues

Rub the inside of the actual fondue pot with the cut side of a garlic clove to add flavor. To help cheese melt quickly, grate or crumble it, and heat it gently because it burns easily.

Oil fondues

Check the temperature of the oil with a cook's thermometer. The temperature should be 190°C/375°F. Adjust the burner to the highest setting once the oil has been transferred to the pot.

Overheating will cause the oil to break down, resulting in a greasy, foamy mass.

Wine and herb fondues

Pour wine or flavoring liquid into the pot, add the cheese, and set over the flame. Grate or crumble the cheese and cover it with a tight-fitting lid to prevent scorching and evaporating too much liquid.

When the cheese has melted, add more wine until it bubbles as it cooks. Cook over low heat until desired consistency is reached.

Don't let fondue pots overheat -- they will burn the oil in them and become useless. And above all, never leave a pot unattended when it is over the flame.

A word about the wine you use for fondues: The ingredients of the cheese fondue dictate the wine you want to use. The wine choice for hard cheeses (like Gruyère or Emmentaler) is a dry white wine, like a dry Riesling, for example; for medium cheeses (like Emmental or young Alpine cheeses), it is an off-dry wine, such as Pinot Gris, Spätlese or Gewürztraminer; for soft cheeses like Raclette or Brunost -- you choose a sweet wine, like a German Riesling or a late harvest wine.

Fondue is a Swiss cultural icon, so if you want to cook fondue, go ahead and use the alcohol used in Switzerland -- kirsch (cherry-flavored eaux-de-vie), cognac, or grappa. And don`t forget the obligatory sliver of green apple for the accompanying Kirschwasser (cherry liqueur) that goes well with darker and sweeter wines.

Beer Fondue

Pour one bottle of beer into the pot. Grate or crumble the cheese and cover it with a tight-fitting lid to prevent scorching and evaporating too much liquid.

When the cheese has melted, add more beer until it bubbles as it cooks. Cook over low heat until desired consistency is reached. The cheese should be firm enough for dipping.

The cheese fondue should be cooked over low or medium heat until it is firm enough to withstand dipping, but the texture should still be creamy. The cheeses suggested for beer fondues are the firmer ones, like Gruyère and Emmentaler.

Dessert Fondues

These are not true fondues in that they do not involve melting cheese, but they are served similarly: on platters with cubes of bread, fruit, cake, or other dessert items.

The main condiment for these is crème fraîche mixed with a small amount of sugar.

Tiny chocolate chips, pâte de frutas (like strawberries, sour apples, and apricots), chopped nuts, and seeds are all delicious flavors for excellent fondues. These are especially good for people who don't eat meat.

Chocolate Fondues

While the generally accepted origin of chocolate fondue is Switzerland, a variety of fondue sets are used in many other countries. These often use a solid chocolate fondue to go with the cheese fondue and non-solid chocolate fondue (usually not of the chocolate bar variety) for the fruit.

The chocolate fondue usually utilizes a bit of white chocolate, but not so much that the fondue is too sweet. Follow the cheese or fruit fondue recipe, except that you can use up to 30 percent white chocolate in the chocolate fondue.

White Chocolate Fondues

Place a small amount of white chocolate in the fondue pot, such as two tablespoons. Cook over low heat until the chocolate is melted. Cook over medium heat until the chocolate fondue is firm enough to withstand dipping, but the texture should still be creamy.

Equipment: The fondue pots of all these types of fondues should be of a higher quality than any other fondue pot.

Chapter 4:

Tips And Tricks And Mistakes To Avoid

Tips and Tricks to Fondue

Fondue recipes are widely varied. You have endless choices of what to make in your fondue pot and what dipping ingredients to prepare. You can even arrange different sauce accompaniments as needed. You practically have an upper hand on making the fondue experience a memorable and gastronomically pleasurable for everyone.

To help you make everything perfect, take a cue from the following tips:

- Never leave out the crust that forms at the bottom of a cheese fondue. In Switzerland, it is called "la religuese" la croute". It is considered a delicacy that is scraped off the pan and served to guests.

- Trim and slice meats before serving. You can even coat it in marinade. If you are dipping meats in a low temp fondue such as a cheese fondue, it is advisable that you precook the meat.

- Give your prepared fruits and vegetables a good squeeze of lemon juice to keep their bright color.

- Prepare raw meats in separate trays so they will not contaminate the other ingredients. Keep them meats chilled in the fridge until you are ready.

- Pat dry meat and vegetables so they will not create dangerous spatters once dipped into hot fondue.

- Meat broths must be consistent with the meat choice: beef on beef broth; chicken on chicken broth.

- Keep a close watch on your fondue pot, especially if it is extremely hot and if children are around.

- The amount of time you must keep your food ingredient dipped onto fondue depends on the type of food you are dipping and the temperature to which you are dipping it in.

- Never use fresh breads or freshly made cakes. They must be at least oneday-old. One-day-old breads and cakes are firm and will not crumble when dipped into fondue.

- Keep fruits chilled before dipping to make sure the sauce stick.

- The ideal proportion is for only about 4 people sharing a fondue pot.

- If hosting a fondue party, make sure that you choose what course you will assign the fondue. Never serve it as an appetizer, main course meal, and dessert all at once.

- Keep the fondue pot only one-thirds full. This is to avoid spattering when people starts to dip their food.

- To decide on how much food to actually prepare for your guests, the rule of thumb is half a pound of food for each person, given that you are serving other entrées as well.

You are so ready to fondue! Let's start!

Mistakes to Avoid When Making Fondue

- Fondue is a meal, not an appetizer or a side dish.

- Fondue is impatient. Bring everyone to the table 5 minutes before the fondue is ready and ask someone to light the lamp and serve the wine.

- 5 (or possibly 6) people per fondue pot Use several pots for large gatherings.

- There are no restrictions. Strings are not formed by cheese fondue. If yours does, something is seriously wrong with your fondue (temperature? wine/cheese proportion?...)

- Drink a lot of cold water. It can make digestion extremely difficult. Take small sips of hot tea or white wine.

- Use or consume red wine. Sacrilege!

- The fondue will be burned/scorched. In addition, with each piece of bread dipped, each guest must contribute to stirring the fondue.

- Scrape the floor. Do not scrape the bottom if it begins to burn; additionally, you want to allow la religieuse to take shape.

- Fruits. Maybe for dessert, but not in the fondue!

- Vegetables. Yes, but only with potatoes, and even then only with fribourgeoise fondue or tomato fondue.

- Bread that is soft. Keep this one for breakfast toasts; use crusty, well-structured bread (baguette).

- If you have company, try not to lick your fork while eating.

- Use reasonable bread pieces; you want to eat cheese, not bread alone!

Chapter 5:

Recipes

---

1.   American Cheeseburger Fondue

This recipe combines all the components of a classic American cheeseburger into a hot cheese fondue that kids and grown-ups alike will love. Dill pickles are an optional add-in to the finished fondue, or you can serve them on the side. Use this recipe as a topping for French fries or a baked potato if you're feeling adventurous.

Serving Size: 4
Preparation Time: 15 minutes
Ingredients:

- 1 tablespoon of extra-virgin olive oil
- ¼ cup of minced white onion
- 1 garlic clove, minced
- 8 ounces of lean ground beef
- 1 teaspoon of prepared yellow mustard
- 1 teaspoon of hamburger seasoning
- ¾ cup of chicken stock, plus more as needed
- 1 tablespoon of cornstarch
- 6 ounces of American cheese
- 8 ounces of grated sharp Cheddar cheese
- ⅓ cup of dill pickles, finely diced (optional)
- Freshly ground black pepper

Directions:

- Combine the onion, garlic, ground beef, yellow mustard, and hamburger seasoning in a bowl. With clean hands, form the mixture into four patties and set them aside. Heat oil in a medium saucepan and add the patties. Cook for about 4 minutes, turning the burgers to ensure even browning on all sides.
- Add the chicken stock, and bring the mixture to a boil. Reduce heat and add the cornstarch to the saucepan, moving the saucepan over low heat. When the sauce begins to thicken, lower the heat to medium-low and stir until the cornstarch is completely dissolved.
- Add the cheese to the sauce and stir until melted. Add the diced pickles and additional chicken stock if the fondue is too thick.
- season with freshly ground black pepper.

2.   *Canadian Maple-Bacon Fondue*

Nothing can replace the sweet and woodsy flavor of pure maple syrup, an iconic match for smoky bacon. Aged white Cheddar pulls all these flavors together into a savory cheese fondue that's perfect for your next weekend brunch menu. Serve with roasted sweet potatoes, mini pancakes, and breakfast sausage.

Serving Size: 4
Preparation Time: 15 minutes
Ingredients:

- ¾ cup of milk, plus more as needed
- 1 tablespoon of cornstarch
- 12 ounces of grated 1-year aged white Cheddar cheese
- 4 ounces of grated mild Gouda cheese
- ¼ cup of pure maple syrup
- 4 bacon slices, cooked and finely chopped
- Freshly ground black pepper

Directions:

- In a large-sized saucepan, combine the milk and cornstarch. Bring to a simmer over medium heat and whisk until thickened. Reduce the heat to low.
- Add the cheeses to the hot milk and stir until the cheese melts and the fondue is smooth.
- Stir in the maple syrup and bacon. Season with pepper.
- Transfer to a fondue pot set to medium heat. If the fondue begins to thicken, add a splash of milk.

3. Fig and Pecan Cheese Fondue

Not only is this a flavorsome fondue but it also has lots of crunch and texture.

Serving Size: 6
Preparation Time: 40 minutes
Ingredients:

- ½ cup of dry white wine
- ½ cup of fig preserves
- ¼ cup of toasted pecans (ground)
- 1 tablespoon of fresh lemon juice
- 2 cups of gruyere cheese (grated)
- 2 cups of Emmental cheese (grated)
- 2 tablespoons of cornstarch
- ¼ teaspoons of black pepper
- Nutmeg (to sprinkle)
- Suggested dippers:
- Sourdough bread (cubed)
- Pumpernickel bread (cubed)

Directions:

- In a medium-sized saucepan over moderate heat, combine the white wine with the fig preserves, ground pecans, and freshly squeezed lemon juice.
- Cook, while frequently stirring, until the preserves melt.
- Combine the grated cheeses along with the black pepper, cornstarch, and a sprinkle of nutmeg.
- Gradually, one handful at a time, stir the cheese mixture into the fig preserve mixture. Make sure that the ingredients are incorporated and melted after each addition.
- Do not allow the fondue to boil.
- Transfer the prepared cheese mixture to a fondue pot, and keep warm, while occasionally stirring.
- Serve with dippers of choice.

4. *French Onion Broth Fondue*

A mention of French onion soup is usually followed closely by a chorus of swooning chatter. Everyone loves the combination of slowly caramelized onions and rich, meaty beef broth with a boozy hint of Cognac. Make sure to serve this recipe with lots of baguettes and Gruyère cheese to satisfy all your French onion soup cravings.

Serving Size: 4
Preparation Time: 55 minutes
Ingredients:

- 1 tablespoon of salted butter
- 1 tablespoon of extra-virgin olive oil
- 1 large yellow onion, thinly sliced
- 4 shallots, peeled and thinly sliced
- 2 garlic cloves, minced
- 2 bay leaves
- 3 fresh thyme sprigs
- 1 ½ teaspoons of white sugar
- 1 teaspoon of kosher salt, plus more for actual seasoning
- ½ teaspoon of freshly ground black pepper
- 1 to 2 tablespoons of Cognac or brandy (optional)
- ½ cup of dry white wine
- 8 cups of beef broth
- 2 pounds of cubed or sliced raw meats, like beef, lamb, venison, bison, pork, chicken, and turkey
- 3 or 4 additional dippers of your choice
- Sauces of your choice

Directions:

- In a medium saucepan, combine the butter, olive oil, onion, shallots, garlic, bay leaves, thyme, sugar, salt, and pepper and sweat over medium-low heat. Stir regularly for approximately about 25 to 30 minutes, or until the onions have evenly caramelized.
- While the broth simmers, arrange the various dippers and sauces around the fondue pot.
- Transfer the hot broth to a fondue pot set to medium-high heat.
- Skewer your chosen item on a fondue fork and place it in the hot broth. Once the item is cooked through, slide it off the fondue fork and onto a plate. Season with additional salt and sauces.

5. *Gouda and Onion Fondue*

This is a classic Dutch fondue dish that is made typically during the holiday season. Served with pretzels and vegetables, this is a delicious and exotic fondue dish you can make any day of the week.

Serving Size: 8
Preparation Time: 40 minutes
Ingredients:

- 4 ounces of pancetta, thick sliced
- 1 red onion, thinly sliced
- 1 teaspoon of ground cumin
- Dash of salt and black pepper
- 1 pound of Gouda
- 2 tablespoons of white flour
- ¾ cup of Riesling
- 8 pretzels, soft
- Rye bread, cut into cubes and for dipping

Directions:

• In a large skillet, occasionally stirring over medium heat, cook pancetta until golden brown, 5 to 7 minutes. Add red onion and cook until onion is translucent 5 to 7 minutes. Add cumin; season with salt and pepper.

• Spread 1 cup of grated cheese over the bottom and sides of an oven-proof dish.

• Add flour; stir in Riesling to coat cheese, then whisk until smooth. Add pancetta-onion mixture and minced buffalo-milk Gouda to the sauce; stir, then season to taste.

• Pour sauce over cheese; top with remaining Gouda. Bake at 400 degrees until golden brown and crispy, 5 to 7 minutes. Serve warm with pretzels and rice crackers.

6. Lemon and Garlic Broth Fondue

Within 25 minutes, you can combine the ingredients of this recipe into a tasty fondue. The lemon and garlic flavor will leave a refreshing aftertaste once you finish eating.

Serving Size: 4
Preparation Time: 45 minutes
Ingredients:

- 2 scallions, white and green parts, sliced
- 1 large garlic clove, sliced
- 1 tablespoon of extra virgin olive oil
- 1 tablespoon of fresh oregano leaves, chopped
- 8 ⅓ cups of chicken broth
- 1 teaspoon of kosher salt, plus more for seasoning
- ⅓ cup of lemon juice, freshly squeezed, plus more as needed
- 2 large eggs
- 2 pounds of raw meats, like beef, lamb, pork, chicken, turkey, and mixed seafood, cubed or sliced
- 4 additional dippers of your choice
- 1 cup of sauces of your choice

Directions:

- In a medium saucepan over medium-high heat, saute the onions and the garlic in the oil until the coloring of the onions is translucent, approximately 5 minutes.
- Add the fresh herbs and stir. Next, add the chicken broth, salt, and lemon juice and bring to a boil.
- Crack the eggs into a small bowl and pour them into the hot broth—Cook for 5 minutes.
- Use tongs to remove the eggs from the broth. Toss them in the same small bowl with lemon juice, salt, and pepper.
- Keep the heat on low, and add the meat. Serve with the egg mixture.
- Add the sauce of your choice and stir. You can use this recipe as the base if you'd like to make several non-meat-flavored broth dips. Add garlic, lemon, or dried herbs. Pour the hot broth over the ingredients, or toss in the ingredients and serve cold or hot after dipping into the broth.
- Invite your friends to come to your house so you can serve them the fondue. Enjoy the time with your friends.

7. Smoked Mozzarella Cheese Fondue

This is a delicious and filling fondue dish you can make whenever you are craving something cheesy. Serve with toasted bread for the tastiest results.

Serving Size: 8
Preparation Time: 30 minutes
Ingredients:

- 8 ounces of cream cheese, soft
- 1 cup of smoked mozzarella cheese
- 1 cup of provolone cheese
- ½ cup of grated Parmesan cheese
- 1/3 cup of sour cream
- ½ teaspoon of dried thyme
- ½ teaspoon of Italian seasoning
- ¼ teaspoon of crushed red pepper flakes
- Dash of salt and black pepper
- 1 tomato, chopped
- 1 tablespoon of parsley, chopped

Directions:

- Preheat the oven to 350 degrees.
- In a bowl, add the soft cream cheese, smoked mozzarella cheese, provolone cheese, grated Parmesan cheese, sour cream, dried thyme, Italian seasoning and crushed red pepper flakes. Stir well until smooth in consistency.
- Season with a dash of salt and black pepper.
- Transfer into a cast iron skillet.
- Place into the oven to bake for 20 to 25 minutes.
- Remove. Serve with a garnish of the chopped tomatoes and chopped parsley.

8.   *Swiss Tomato Fondue*

Here is another classic Swiss fondue made extra delightful with tomatoes, garlic, and shallots. It stays true to the original fondue recipe but adds in some other ingredients to give it a twist. It's a great recipe for dipping not just breads but also fresh vegetables like carrots and radishes among many others.

Serving Size: 24
Preparation Time: 40 minutes
Ingredients:

- 1 pound of Gruyere cheese, grated
- 8 ounces of Emmental cheese, grated
- 3 pieces of tomatoes, seeded and chopped
- 2 garlic cloves, minced
- 1 pieces of shallot, minced
- 12 ounces of dry white wine
- 2 tablespoons of butter

Directions:

- Reserve ⅓ of Gruyere for the fondue and then melt the rest with the wine in the fondue pot.
- In a small saucepan, add the garlic, shallots, and tomatoes and sauté until tomatoes become soft, about 5 minutes. Add in the cheese, pepper, and salt in small portions and begin melting the cheese. Do not overheat the fondue, or it will start congealing.
- Mince the shallots, and garlic and then fry them with the butter and wine. When the fondue has taken on a nice taste and begun to melt, add the chopped tomato. Continue to cook for about 15 minutes. Turn off the heat and then, remove a small portion of the fondue and check the taste.
- Add the remaining cheese and continue cooking until the fondue is almost melted. Do not reheat and instead allow it to cool. Serve with fresh fruit, vegetables, or bread.

9.   Baked Brie Fondue

Combine the sweet and savory flavors of a classic baked Brie dish by adding fig jam and smoky bacon to this rich fondue. Serve this decadent Brie fondue with an array of sweet and savory dippers like grapes and apples, baguettes, and steamed squash and potatoes.

Serving Size: 4
Preparation Time: 10 minutes
Ingredients:

- ¾ cup of dry white wine, plus more as needed
- 1 tablespoon of cornstarch
- 1 pound of Brie cheese, rind removed and cut into ¼-inch cubes
- ¼ cup of fig jam
- ¼ cup of crumbled, cooked bacon

Directions:

- In a medium saucepan over medium heat, combine the wine and the cornstarch. Stir until the cornstarch is dissolved, then add the cubed Brie and stir to combine, making sure not to let the fondue get too hot.
- Bring the mixture to a simmer over medium heat and cook until the Brie is evenly cooked and the mixture is thickened about 5 to 10 minutes.
- Remove the fondue from the heat and stir in the fig jam and crumbled bacon. Serve immediately with plenty of crackers or croutons.

10. Basil Pesto Fondue

Basil pesto is an herbaceous mix of nuts, garlic, Parmesan, and fresh basil that adds a punch of refreshing flavor to an otherwise heavy dish. This fondue is particularly suited for dipping precooked ravioli and tortellini and a selection of fresh and lightly grilled vegetables.

Serving Size: 4
Preparation Time: 10 minutes
Ingredients:

- 2 cups of fresh basil leaves
- 2 garlic cloves, crushed
- ¼ cup of extra-virgin olive oil
- 2 tablespoons of pine nuts, toasted
- 2 tablespoons of Parmesan cheese
- 2 teaspoons of freshly squeezed lemon juice, divided
- Kosher salt
- Freshly ground black pepper
- 1 cup of dry white wine or chicken stock, plus more as needed
- 4 teaspoons of cornstarch
- 8 ounces of grated Gruyère cheese
- 8 ounces of grated Fontina cheese

Directions:

- Stew the basil and garlic with a little olive oil in a medium saucepan on low flame in a large skillet. When it is aromatic and starts to turn a bit color, add the pine nuts and toss to coat. Add half of the Parmesan and stir and then add the rest of the cheese and the lemon juice, followed by the wine. Stir the mixture and cook for about 5 minutes. In a large bowl, dissolve the 2 teaspoons of cornstarch in cool water. Stir the cornstarch slurry into the pan and cook for another 2 or 3 minutes. Add the grated cheese to the pan and cook for another 2 minutes.
- Remove from heat and dice the fondue. Transfer the fondue to a fondue pot or sauce pot. Heat and stir in a fondue burner and serve. For an extra lavish meal, garnish the fondue with basil-stuffed sausages.

11. Blue Cheese and Leek Fondue

Cheddar cheese and mild Gouda form a rich and creamy foundation, and a liberal crumble of blue cheese is added on top. Pair with a pint or two of malty stout to be transported to a pub in the British countryside.

Serving Size: 4
Preparation Time: 15 minutes
Ingredients:

- 1 large leek, green leaves removed, cleaned and diced
- 1 tablespoon of salted butter
- ¾ cup of beer, plus more as needed
- 1 tablespoon of cornstarch
- 10 ounces of grated 1-year aged white Cheddar cheese
- 6 ounces of grated mild Gouda cheese
- 1 teaspoon of Worcestershire sauce
- 2 ounces of strong blue cheese, crumbled

Directions:

- In a skillet, combine the diced leek, salted butter and a splash of beer over medium heat. Cook until the leeks are soft, stirring occasionally. When the leeks are finished, transfer them to a mixing bowl. Add in the cornstarch and allow to thicken for about ten minutes. Don't over-thicken.
- In a deep skillet, heat up the additional beer, over medium-low heat. Add in the blue cheese, Gouda, and Worcestershire sauce. Cook for about ten minutes.
- When the cheese is done, stir in the Cheddar, Gouda, and Worcestershire sauce. Stir until the cheese is well incorporated, and the mixture is smooth.
- If the fondue is too thick, add some additional beer slowly until you get the right consistency.
- Serve immediately

12. Smoky Three Cheese Fondue

This is a cheesy fondue dish you can make if you are looking for a fondue dish that is versatile. Serve this fondue with fresh fruit, vegetables or whatever seared meat you desire.

Serving Size: 6
Preparation Time: 30 minutes
Ingredients:

- 12 ounces of smoked gouda cheese, cut into cubes
- 8 ounces of gruyere cheese, cut into cubes
- 4 ounces of Swiss cheese, cut into cubes
- 2 tablespoons of cornstarch
- ½ teaspoon of cayenne pepper
- 1 clove of garlic, minced
- 1 ½ cups of dried white wine
- 1 tablespoon of brandy
- 1 tablespoon of truffle oil
- Dash of grated nutmeg
- Steak, cut into cubes and cooked, for serving
- Assorted vegetables, for serving
- Ingredients for the croissants:
- 6 croissants, sliced into sticks
- 6 tablespoons of butter, soft
- 2 cloves of garlic, grated
- ¼ cup of basil, chopped

Directions:

- Prepare the fondue. In a bowl, add in the cubes of smoked gouda, gruyere and swiss cheeses. Add in the cornstarch and cayenne pepper. Toss well to coat.
- Rub the inside of a fondue por with garlic. Toss out the garlic.
- In the fondue pot, add in the dried white wine, brandy and truffle oil. Stir well to mix and set over low to medium heat.
- Once the wine mix begins to bubble, add in the coated cheese. Cook for 3 minutes or until melted.
- Add in the grated nutmeg and dash of black pepper.
- Prepare the croissants. In a bowl, add in the butter, grated garlic and chopped basil. Stir well to mix. Spread this mix on both sides of the croissants.
- In a skillet set over medium heat, add in the croissants. Cook for approximately about 3 to 4 minutes on each side or until toasted.
- Serve the croissants with the fondue.

13. Traditional Swiss Fondue

The original recipe for Swiss cheese fondue was simply local wine and cheese melted together and served warm with cubes of fresh bread. Cornstarch, popularized in the early 1900s, created a smooth, consistent cheese fondue. This classic recipe will satisfy your desire for a pot of bubbling cheese fondue.

Serving Size: 4
Preparation Time: 15 minutes
Ingredients:

- 1 garlic clove, halved
- ¾ cup of dry white wine, plus more as needed
- 8 ounces of grated Gruyère cheese
- 8 ounces of grated Emmentaler cheese
- 1 tablespoon of cornstarch
- Freshly squeezed lemon juice
- 1 tablespoon of kirsch (optional)
- Freshly ground black pepper

Directions:

- Rub the inside of a ceramic, ovenproof fondue pot (or a small saucepan with enamel, stainless steel, or cast iron insert) with the garlic and discard the garlic.
- Make a roux by mixing wine and cornstarch. Pour the wine into a fondue pot. Stir constantly until the wine is warm and the cornstarch has dissolved.
- Over a low flame, add the cheese and stir until melted, thinning with additional wine or broth if needed. Add the lemon juice and kirsch, if desired.
- Serving: Transfer the melted cheese to a fondue pot and serve with chunks of bread and potatoes.

14.   Champagne Fondue

Make this delicious fondue whenever you want to surprise your significant other with something special.

Serving Size: 4
Preparation Time: 5 minutes
Ingredients:

- 2 cups of champagne
- 1 clove of garlic, minced
- 1 pound of swiss cheese, shredded
- 3 tablespoons of all-purpose flour
- 1 tablespoon of lemon juice
- 1 tablespoon of Kirsch, optional
- ¼ teaspoon of white pepper
- Dash of salt
- Dash of nutmeg

Directions:

- Rub the clove of garlic around the inside of the fondue pot. Add into the fondue pot.
- Add in the Kirsch, white pepper, dash of salt and dash of nutmeg. Stir well to mix.
- Cook for 5 minutes or until the cheese is melted.
- Serve.

15. Cheese and Tomato Fondue

The tangy flavor from tomatoes is what gives this cheese dish a characteristic taste you will love. Try it with some breadsticks or French bread.

Serving Size: 24
Preparation Time: 20 minutes
Ingredients:

- 1 ounces of butter
- 2 garlic cloves, pressed
- ½ teaspoon of onion, minced
- 3 small seeded tomatoes, chopped
- 12 ounces of dry white wine
- 16 ounces of gruyere cheese, shredded
- 8 ounces of Swiss cheese, shredded

Directions:

- In a small mixing bowl, combine butter, garlic and onions
- In a cheese fondue pot or a heavy bottomed saucepan, combine cheese and wine
- When cheese melts, in the pot, slowly add the mixture made in the mixing bowl
- Allow cheese to melt, stirring it with a long serving fork
- Transfer to a fondue pot or dip bread in it

Note: When the cheese gets solid, you can add the tomatoes and cheese mixture to make the fondue creamier and tastier. When the cheese gets thin, add cheese and wine.

16. Cheesy Squash Fondue

Some cheesy goodness works well with the slightly sweet taste of squash. It feels like heaven in your mouth, especially when you dunk it spinach and artichokes into the mix. Imagine the gooey cheese texture made flavorful with squash and bits of chunky goodness from spinach and artichoke? Sounds appetizing, right?

Serving Size: 4
Preparation Time: 1 hour 25 minutes
Ingredients:

- 2 cups of Gruyere cheese, freshly grated
- 2 ounces of Neufchatel cheese
- 2 pieces of acorn squash, halved crosswise and seeds removed
- 4 ounces of fresh spinach, chopped
- 7 ounces of artichoke hearts, drained
- 2 tablespoons of butter
- 1 cup of half-and-half
- Salt and pepper to taste
- 1 piece of baguette loaf, sliced

Directions:

- Preheat the oven to a heat of 400 degrees F. Prepare a baking dish lined with foil.
- Arrange squash halves onto prepared pan. Sprinkle some salt and pepper. Set aside.
- Melt butter in a pan over medium fire and sauté chopped spinach until slightly wilted.
- Add artichoke hearts and continue sautéing for 3 minutes more.
- Transfer mixture to a bowl and mix together with half-and-half, plus Neufchatel cheese until blended. Scoop onto squash halves, keeping them ¾ full.
- Cover top with grated Gruyere cheese. Place a prepared sheet of aluminum foil on the baking pan to cover the squash. Bake in preheated oven for an hour.
- After an hour, remove foil, turn up the temperature, and cook for another 5 minutes, until top is brown and the cheese is bubbly.
- Serve cheesy squash fondue in separate plates with sliced baguette.

17. Classic Meat Fondue

The real secret to a successful meat fondue party is on the dipping sauces, really. It is best that you prepare a handful of choices so your guests could decide for themselves whether to go for sweet, tangy, salty, spicy, or any taste they might prefer. That said, you must not take for granted how delightfully prepared the fondue itself must be. Plus, make sure that the meat is super fresh. You can never go wrong with that.

Serving Size: 4

Preparation Time: 30 minutes

Ingredients:

- 2 pounds of beef tenderloin, sliced into 1-inch strips
- 1 liter of vegetable oil
- 1 cup of crusty white bread, sliced
- 2 cups of green salad

Directions:

- Fill the fondue pot halfway through with oil.
- Light the heating element on medium and keep the oil temperature at around 375 degrees F.
- Place meat and bread in different serving plates together with small bowls of different sauces.
- Provide your guests with a fondue fork each and let them dunk their meat onto hot oil.

18. Hot Queso Fondue

The Tex-Mex origins of Queso Fundido and hot Queso dip straddle the border of the Southern United States and Northern Mexico. Although these two hot cheese dips differ in many ways—one is simply cheese and chiles melted in a hot skillet, and the other is a creamy mixture of cheeses and roasted poblanos—they share many of the same flavors. This recipe combines the best qualities of both dishes into one hot and oozy creamy cheese fondue, with garnishes of chorizo, chiles, fresh cilantro, and tomatoes.

Serving Size: 4
Preparation Time: 15 minutes
Ingredients:

- 2 tablespoons of tequila
- ¾ cup of light beer, plus more as needed
- 1 garlic clove, minced
- 1 tablespoon of cornstarch
- ½ cup of American cheese
- 10 ounces of grated Monterey Jack cheese
- 3 ounces of grated Oaxaca cheese
- ½ cup of crumbled chorizo, fried until crispy
- ¼ cup of roasted green chile peppers, drained and chopped
- 2 tablespoons of fresh cilantro, chopped
- 2 tablespoons of seeded and diced tomato

Directions:

- Combine the tequila, beer, and garlic in a medium saucepan and bring to a simmer, using a whisk to create an even mixture. Reduce until there is enough liquid to cover the bottom of a fondue pot or a medium-sized saucepan.
- Whisk together the cornstarch and a couple of tablespoons of water in a separate bowl. Whisk the mixture into the saucepan. Slowly pour the cheese, a little at a time, whisking constantly. The mixture will begin to thicken. Additional beer can be added as needed, a tablespoon at a time, to achieve the desired consistency, which should be creamy with a little texture.
  - Transfer the cheese to the fondue pot, set over a slow flame, and serve with all of the garnishes.

19. Mushroom Broth Fondue

Dried mushrooms are the star of the show in this rich and flavorful mushroom broth. When steeped in hot water, dried mushrooms release myriad earthy, meaty, and umami flavors. This full-bodied vegetable-based broth can be a smart choice for the vegan and vegetarian crowd, but it works equally well for cooking your favorite meats.

Serving Size: 4
Preparation Time: 50 minutes
Ingredients:

- 4 cups of water
- 1 cup of dried porcini mushrooms
- ½ small onion, cut into chunks
- 1 garlic clove, crushed
- 3 fresh thyme sprigs
- 1 tablespoon of extra-virgin olive oil
- 4 ¼ cups of vegetable broth
- 1 tablespoon of soy sauce
- 1 teaspoon of sherry vinegar
- 1 teaspoon of kosher salt, plus more for actual seasoning
- ½ teaspoon of freshly ground black pepper
- ½ cup of cremini mushrooms, thinly sliced
- 2 pounds of cubed or sliced raw meats, like beef, lamb, pork, chicken, turkey, and mixed seafood
- 2 pounds of mixed mushrooms and vegetables (vegan option)
- 3 or 4 additional dippers of your choice
- Sauces of your choice

Directions:

- Pour the water into a small pot over medium heat. Add the dried porcini mushrooms and allow the mushrooms to steep in the water like a tea for approximately about 10 minutes.
- In a separate large saucepan, sauté the onion, garlic, and thyme in the olive oil over medium heat for approximately about 2 to 3 minutes until the ingredients begin to caramelize. Add the vegetable broth, soy sauce, sherry vinegar, salt, pepper, and mushroom "tea" to the pot, and bring to a simmer over low heat for approximately about 30 minutes.
- Once ready, strain the broth through a fine-mesh strainer, and return the broth to the saucepan, discarding the aromatics.
- Add the sliced mushrooms to the broth and simmer for approximately about 2 to 3 minutes. Check the broth for seasoning and adjust if necessary.
- While the broth simmers, arrange the various dippers and sauces around the fondue pot.
- Transfer the hot broth to a fondue pot set to medium-high heat.
- Skewer your chosen item on a fondue fork and place it in the hot broth. Once the item is cooked through, slide it off the fondue fork onto a plate. Season with salt and sauces.

20. Pizza Fondue

Make this savory fondue dish whenever you have a kitchen full of picky eaters in your home. It tastes just like pizza, I know everyone in your home will love it.

Serving Size: 5
Preparation Time: 15 minutes
Ingredients:

- 1 pound of lean ground chuck
- 1 onion, chopped
- 1 to 2 cloves of garlic, minced
- 2, 10 ounces cans of pizza sauce
- 1 ½ cups of cheddar cheese, shredded
- 1 cup of mozzarella cheese, shredded
- French bread, cut into cubes

Directions:

- Crumble the lean ground chuck and place into a colander.
- Add in the chopped onion and minced garlic. Stir well to mix.
- In a saucepan set over medium to high heat, add in the ground chuck. Cook for approximately about 8 to 10 minutes or until browned. Transfer into a fondue pot.
- In the fondue pot, add in the cans of pizza sauce, shredded cheddar cheese and shredded mozzarella cheese.
- Cook for 5 minutes or until the cheese melts.
- Serve with the French bread cubes.

21. Shrimps and Scallops Fondue

A decadent fondue loaded with seafood is definitely irresistible. It's a perfect dinner date idea for couples who just want to spend time together over a light but very filling meal coupled with a good glass of wine. What's even more exciting with this dish is that, you don't have to stick to just shrimps and scallops. You may add in a few seafood choices as well, including crabmeat, lobster, or flaked fish. Let your imagination run wild.

Serving Size: 4
Preparation Time: 30 minutes
Ingredients:

- 1 pound of shrimp, peeled and deveined
- 12 ounces of scallops, chopped
- 16 ounces of Monterey Jack cheese
- 2 cups of mushrooms, sliced
- ½ cup of green onions, diced
- 2 cups of spinach leaves
- 1 ½ cups of onion, diced
- 2 tablespoons of garlic, minced
- 10 tablespoons of butter, divided
- 1 ½ cups of organic white wine
- 1 ½ cups of cream
- 6 tablespoons of flour
- 1 teaspoon of sea salt
- 1 tablespoon of Cajun seasoning
- 1 piece of crusty sourdough, cut into 1-inch cubes

Directions:

- Melt 2 tablespoons of butter in a pan on high heat.
- Add shrimps and scallops, sprinkle with salt and Cajun seasoning, and stir for about 5 minutes.
- Turn heat to medium and add mushrooms, spinach, green onions, and garlic. Continue to stir until spinach is slightly wilted. Transfer to a fondue pot and set aside.
- Heat remaining prepared butter in the same pan over medium fire and sauté onion for about 2 minutes until translucent.
- Pour wine and simmer on low heat for about 7 minutes.
- Whisk in cream and cheeses and season with some salt. Allow cheeses to melt, stirring frequently for approximately about 5 minutes more.
- Pour fondue onto prepared pot with seafood and veggies, place heat source on low, and stir to blend.
- Serve with bread cubes.

22. Salted Caramel Fondue

This fondue is a dish that is equally entertaining and delicious. Serve with your friends on a chilly night.

Serving Size: 4
Preparation Time: 15 minutes
Ingredients:

- 1 cup of white sugar
- 6 tablespoons (¾ stick) salted butter
- ⅓ cup of heavy whipping cream
- 1 teaspoon of kosher salt

Directions:

- Using a saucepan, set over medium low heat, add the sugar and allow it to melt as you stir with a wooden spoon. Clumps will form from the sugar and later melt to form a thick liquid (amber in color) as you continue stirring, but keep a close eye on it as it can burn quickly.
- Once the sugar has completely melted and is a golden amber color, immediately add the butter. The caramel starts bubbling rapidly. If the butter separates as you whisk, don't worry. It will still come together.
- Slowly add in the cream as you stir.
- Transfer to a fondue pot and set to low heat, or allow to cool completely and refrigerate for even 1 month.

23. Spiced Oil Fondue

This is the authentic French-style fondue. It's just mostly oil, flavored with a couple of spices to provide a subtle effect into your taste buds. Apart from vegetables, you can also use meat as your dipping ingredient. You may also add bread into the equation to make a main course meal that you can serve to friends over a special, intimate dinner.

Serving Size: 6

Preparation Time: 20 minutes

Ingredients:

- ¾ cup of olive oil
- 12 pieces of anchovy fillets
- 6 garlic cloves, chopped
- 6 tablespoons of unsalted butter, at room temperature
- 3 cups of assorted vegetables, cut into bite-size pieces
- 1 piece of crusty French bread loaf, cut into 1-inch cubes
- 1 ½ cups of skinless and boneless chicken breasts, cubed and boiled

Directions:

- Combine oil, anchovies, garlic, and butter in a food processor. Pulse until smooth.
- Heat mixture in a pan over low fire, stirring occasionally for about 15 minutes.
- Transfer into a fondue pot, keeping the oil temperature steady by putting a heat source on low.
- Serve with vegetables, bread, and meat for dipping.

24. Toffee Fondue

This is the perfect fondue dish for you to make whenever you need a special and classy fondue dish for your next dinner party.

Serving Size: 4

Preparation Time: 5 minutes

Ingredients:

- ½ cup of butter
- 2 cups of dark brown sugar
- 1 cup of white corn syrup
- 2 tablespoons of water
- 1, 14 ounce can of sweet and condensed milk
- 1 teaspoon of pure vanilla

Directions:

- In a double boiler with the bottom half containing simmering water, add in the butter to the top portion. Allow to melt.
- Slowly add in the dark brown sugar, white corn syrup, water, condensed milk and pure vanilla. Whisk well until smooth in consistency.
- Cook for 3 minutes or until thick in consistency.
- Pour the mix into a fondue pot and keep warm.
- Serve with sliced apples and pears.

25. Wild Mushroom and Herb Fondue

Mushrooms and herbs are the perfect savory partner for melting cheeses like the Gruyère and Fontina featured in this recipe. If you have access to a selection of dried mushrooms like porcinis and chanterelles, simply steep them in hot water for 5 to 10 minutes and drain well before adding them to the other mushrooms.

Serving Size: 4
Preparation Time: 15 minutes
Ingredients:

- 2 tablespoons of extra-virgin olive oil
- 2 cups of mixed cremini, oyster, and shiitake mushrooms, cleaned and cut into ½-inch slices
- 1 teaspoon of fresh rosemary, chopped
- 1 ½ teaspoons of fresh thyme, chopped
- ¼ cup of fresh parsley leaves, chopped
- Kosher salt
- Freshly ground black pepper
- ¾ cup of dry white wine, plus more as needed
- 10 ounces of grated Gruyère cheese
- 6 ounces of grated Fontina cheese
- 4 teaspoons of cornstarch
- Freshly squeezed lemon juice

Directions:

- In a medium sauté pan, warm the olive oil over medium-high heat. Cook the tyme, rosemary, the mushrooms and sauté until cooked through and browned. Add the parsley and season with salt and pepper.
- Simmer the wine to another pan.
- Mix the cornstarch and cheeses, Add the wine to the mixture. Add lemon juice to taste. Stir in the mushrooms.
- Transfer to a fondue pot set to medium heat. If the fondue begins to thicken, add a splash of wine.

26. Bananas Foster Fondue

The classic Bananas Foster recipe originated in New Orleans in the 1950s. In this fondue, all the same great flavors of butter, banana, and dark rum are turned into a sauce for dunking your favorite dessert fondue dippers. Overripe bananas will become mushy when sautéed, so choose a banana that is just starting to ripen for this recipe.

Serving Size: 2
Preparation Time: 10 minutes
Ingredients:

- 1 cup of white sugar
- 7 tablespoons of salted butter, divided
- ⅓ cup of heavy (whipping) cream
- 1 banana, peeled and diced
- 1 tablespoon of brown sugar
- ½ teaspoon of ground cinnamon
- 2 tablespoons of dark rum
- 2 tablespoons of banana liqueur (optional)

Directions:

- In a medium saucepan, melt the white sugar over medium-low heat, stirring occasionally with a high-heat-resistant rubber spatula
- Slowly stir in the cream. The mixture will bubble, but keep stirring. Boil for 1 minute.
- In a small sauté pan, combine the remaining 1 tablespoon of butter, the banana, the brown sugar, and the cinnamon, and sauté over high heat for approximately about 2 minutes, or until everything starts to melt together. Add the rum and banana liqueur (if using) and sauté for approximately about 1 to 2 minutes. Add this mixture to the caramel sauce and stir to combine.
- Transfer to a fondue pot set to low heat, or allow to cool completely and refrigerate for approximately about up to 1 week.

27. Caramel Apple-Brie Fondue

Brie cheese fondue with caramel and apple is a fun addition to your weekend brunch menu. It's not actually too sweet and pairs well with breakfast favorites like waffles, croissants, and fresh fruit. Kick it up a notch by adding chopped pecans and apple brandy.

Serving Size: 4
Preparation Time: 10 minutes
Ingredients:

- 1 tablespoon of salted butter
- ¼ cup of brown sugar
- ¼ teaspoon of ground cinnamon
- 1 apple, peeled, cored, and diced
- 8 ounces of Brie cheese
- ½ teaspoon of cornstarch
- ⅓ cup of heavy (whipping) cream

Directions:

- In a small sauté pan, cook the butter, brown sugar, and cinnamon over medium heat for 3 minutes, or until the butter and sugar come together to form a caramel.
- Add the apple and cook for 5 minutes, or until the apple is softened and the sauce is thickened. Remove from the heat and set aside.
- Scrape the bloomy rind off the Brie cheese using the edge of a spoon. Cut the Brie into cubes and place in a bowl. Add the cornstarch and toss to coat.
- In a small saucepan, warm the cream over medium heat until very hot but not simmering. Add the Brie a few cubes at a time, stirring as they melt into the cream. Transfer to a fondue pot set to low heat.
- Spoon the caramel apple topping onto the Brie fondue and serve immediately.

28. Chocolate-Espresso Fondue

Looking forward to preparing a delicious dessert for your guests to relish? Chocolate – Espresso Fondue is the perfect treat.

Serving Size: 2
Preparation Time: 15 minutes
Ingredients:

- ¼ cup of hot water
- 1 tablespoon of instant espresso
- 2 tablespoons of liqueur (optional)
- ¼ cup of heavy whipping cream
- 1 teaspoon of sugar
- 6 ounces of semisweet chocolate, chopped

Directions:

- In a bowl, mix together the hot water and instant espresso and set aside for 5 minutes. Add the liqueur (if using).
- In a small saucepan, bring the prepared espresso, cream, and sugar to simmer over low heat.
- Transfer to a fondue pot and set to low heat, or allow to cool completely and refrigerate for up to 2 weeks.

29. Luscious Caramel Fondue

With a combination of vanilla bean, cream, and sugar, this recipe develops a luscious tasty caramel that you can serve in varieties of parties and functions. Serve it with dippers, chocolate pound cakes, fresh fruit, or cookies.

Serving Size: 12

Preparation Time: 15 minutes

Ingredients:

- 1 split vanilla bean with the seeds scraped out
- ¼ cup of water
- 1 cup of heavy cream
- 2 cups of granulated sugar
- 1 cup of your favorite dipping ingredients

Directions:

- Combine the water with the sugar in a medium saucepan. Cook on med-low. Stir until the sugar dissolves.
- Cover the pan. Bring to boil. Leave covered for a minute.
- Raise the heat to med-high. Do not stir. Swirl the pan while cooking until the color of the mixture is a darkened amber. Add the cream CAREFULLY as it will splatter.
- Add the vanilla beans. Whisk and combine. Transfer the mixture to your fondue pot. Set over a warming candle. Serve promptly with the assorted dipping ingredients.

30. Red Velvet Fondue

This Red Velvet Fondue is a great dessert idea for a romantic date for two. Whether it's your anniversary or a universal occasion such as Valentine's or even for no reason at all, it's worth going great lengths for putting together a delectable meal that you and your loved one would partake in That could easily make the night truly memorable.

Serving Size: 2
Preparation Time: 25 minutes
Ingredients:

- 1/3 cup of heavy whipping cream
- 4 ounces of milk chocolate, chopped
- 1 tablespoon of coffee liqueur
- 4 drops of red food coloring
- 1 platter of cheesecake, biscuits, fruit and cake

Directions:

- Heat cream in a pan over medium fire.
- Stir in chopped chocolates and coffee liqueur. Mix until completely melted.
- Transfer to a fondue pot heated on low and serve with a platter of treats for dipping.

31. Spiked English Custard Fondue

Custard is the perfect partner for cubes of dense Half-Pound Cake, Crisp Gingersnap Cookies, and fresh fruit. This classic British sweet cream sauce is thickened with egg yolks, which gives it a rich and velvety texture. This recipe calls for a pinch of warm spices and a splash of whiskey, but the combinations of flavors you can add are endless—try adding chocolate, nuts, or your favorite dessert liqueur.

Serving Size: 4
Preparation Time: 10 minutes
Ingredients:

- ¾ cup of whole milk
- ½ cup of heavy (whipping) cream
- ½ teaspoon of vanilla extract
- ¼ teaspoon of ground cinnamon
- ¼ teaspoon of freshly grated nutmeg
- 2 tablespoons of sugar
- 2 large egg yolks
- 1 ½ teaspoons of cornstarch
- 2 tablespoons of whiskey (optional)

Directions:

- In a small saucepan, bring the milk, cream, vanilla, cinnamon, and nutmeg to a simmer over medium heat.
- In a bowl, whisk together the sugar, egg yolks, and cornstarch. Slowly add the prepared hot milk mixture to the egg mixture while whisking constantly.
- Return the mixture to the saucepan over very low heat and stir continuously until just below a simmer. The custard should thicken enough to coat the back of a wooden spoon. Be careful not to scramble the eggs.
- Stir in the whiskey (if using) and transfer to a fondue pot set to low heat, or allow to cool completely and refrigerate for approximately about up to 2 weeks.

32. White Chocolate Fondue

To kick things off, we have a simple yet delicious fondue dish you can serve if you have a craving for decadent chocolate.

Serving Size: 2

Preparation Time: 5 minutes

Ingredients:

- 1 pound of vanilla candy coating
- ½ cup of half and half
- 2 tablespoons of brandy

Directions:

- In a saucepan set over low heat, add in the candy coating. Heat for 1 to 2 minutes or until fully melted.
- Slowly add in the half and half. Stir well until evenly blended.
- Add in the brandy and stir well until incorporated.
- Remove from heat.
- Serve at room temperature with berries or assorted fruits.

Chapter 6:

Recipes for Parties with Family and Friends

33.   Bittersweet Chocolate Fondue

This unconventional mouthwatering dish goes beyond a simple dessert. It brings the whole family and friends together to share food. You can make it as a small party meal or double the amount of it and call more people to come and enjoy it together.

Serving Size: 8
Preparation Time: 10 minutes
Ingredients:

- 2 cups of heavy cream
- 1 pound of bittersweet chocolate, chopped
- 1 cup of desired dipping

Directions:

- Combine the cream and chocolate in a medium sized heat proof bowl set over a pan of gently simmering water.
- Use a wooden spoon to stir now and then until the chocolate has melted and the mixture becomes smooth.
- Divide among eight small ramekins or bowls. Serve with the dipping ingredients.

34. Cheesecake Fondue

This fondue is a delicious dessert when you have a date home or when you want a simple meal for entertaining your friends.

Serving Size: 2
Preparation Time: 10 minutes
Ingredients:

- ½ cup of heavy whipping cream
- ¼ cup of crème fraiche
- ¼ cup of mascarpone cheese
- ½ cup of cream cheese
- 2 tablespoons of sugar
- ½ teaspoon of vanilla extract
- ⅛ teaspoon of ground cinnamon
- ¼ cup of white chocolate chips

Directions:

- In a small saucepan, combine the cream, crème fraiche, mascarpone cheese, cream cheese, sugar, vanilla extract, and cinnamon.
- Bring to simmer over low heat, stirring until you get a smooth consistency. Remove from the heat.
- Add the white chocolate chips and stir to combine. Make sure the chocolate chips are melted, and transfer to a fondue pot set to low heat, or allow to cool completely and refrigerate for up to 1 week.

35. Chocolate Mint Fondue

This fondue is everything you need for a dinner party dessert. The dark color and chocolate flavor tell all about the great recipe.

Serving Size: 6

Preparation Time: 15 minutes

Ingredients:

- ½ cup of heavy cream
- 12 ounces of dark chocolate, chopped
- 3 tablespoons of mint chocolate liqueur or crème de menthe

Directions:

- Using your double boiler, mix the chocolate and heavy cream. Heat as you stir until fully melted.
- Transfer to a warm fondue pot.
- Add the mint chocolate liqueur; stir to incorporate.
- Keep the fondue warm over low heat and serve with fresh fruit, cookies, or marshmallows.

36. Cinnamon Roll Fondue

This is party food at its finest! It's a simple cream cheese dipping sauce that is best served with cinnamon rolls. You can add other treats as your dipping ingredients, like one-day old cakes, brownies, cookies, mallows, crackers, and bread sticks. The flavor is just oh-so-yummy. Perfect to perk up your mood instantly.

Serving Size: 6
Preparation Time: 2 hours 20 minutes
Ingredients:

- 1-8 ounces package cream cheese, at room temperature
- Pinch of cinnamon
- 2 cups of powdered sugar
- ½ cup of butter, at room temperature
- 1 ½ teaspoon of vanilla extract

Directions:

- Combine cream cheese, cinnamon, butter, and vanilla in a mixer. Beat until smooth.
- Gradually add sugar and mix until well combined.
- Transfer mixture in a slow cooker and cook on low for an hour and a half, stirring occasionally.
- Pour fondue in a fondue pot and heat on low to keep it warm.
- Serve with bite-size cinnamon rolls and other treats.

37. Creamy Raspberry Fondue

This is a combination of whipped cream and raspberries offering a refreshing taste for a decadent and delicious party dessert.

Serving Size: 5
Preparation Time: 20 minutes
Ingredients:

- 2 (10 ounces) packs thawed frozen raspberries
- ¼ cup of cornstarch
- ½ cup of cold water
- 1 (4 ounces) tub whipped cream cheese, room temperature
- 2 tablespoons of granulated sugar
- ¼ cup of brandy
- 1 cup of fresh fruit and cake cubes to serve

Directions:

- In a pan, using the back of a wooden spoon, slightly crush the raspberries.
- In a bowl, blend the cornstarch with the water and add the raspberries.
- Cook while stirring until thickened and bubbly.
- Sieve the mixture with a fine mesh sieve and discard the seeds.
- Transfer the prepared mixture to a fondue pot and set over the fondue burner.
- Add the cream cheese stirring well until entirely melted.
- Stir in the sugar, while a little at a time, adding the brandy.
- Serve with the fresh fruit and cake cubes.

38. Irish Cheddar Fondue

In 20 minutes, you can make this delicious dish for your home event. It is tasty and very easy to prepare.

Serving Size: 6
Preparation Time: 20 minutes
Ingredients:

- 1 garlic clove, cut into halves
- 1 cup of dried white wine
- 1 ½ tablespoon of cornstarch
- 1 ½ pound of Irish cheddar cheese, shredded
- 2 tablespoons of Irish whiskey
- Dash sea salt
- Dash black pepper

Directions:

- Rub the garlic along the bottom and sides of a saucepan. Set over low to medium heat. Toss out the garlic.
- Add the dried white wine to the saucepan. Allow to simmer.
- In a bowl, add in the shredded cheddar cheese and cornstarch. Toss well to coat. Add to the saucepan. Stir well to mix. Cook for 5 minutes or until smooth.
- Add in the Irish whiskey and continue to cook for 1 to 2 minutes.
- Season with a dash of salt and black pepper.
- Remove from the heat and serve immediately.

39. Matcha Fondue

This fondue creates a green color which contributes to the color variation on your dining table. Serve it with relevant dippers like cake pieces, and everybody at your party will fight for it.

Serving Size: 3

Preparation Time: 15 minutes

Ingredients:

- 8 ounces of white chocolate, chopped
- ½ cup of heavy cream
- 1 teaspoon of cooking grade matcha
- 1 cup of cake pieces, marshmallows, strawberries, pretzel rods, etc. for dipping

Directions:

- Add the matcha to a saucepan. Add 1 tbsp. of the cream and stir to combine. Stir well until you get rid of the lumps. Now add the remaining cream.
- Add the chocolate and melt over medium low constantly stirring.
- Pour into a fondue pot.
- Serve with the dippers and enjoy!

40. Swiss Cheese Fondue

There's no better way to start this fondue cookbook than with this traditional Swiss cheese fondue. It's a combination of three different and delectable Swiss cheeses: Gruyere, Raclette, and Emmental. The original recipe calls for wine but if you want to make your fondue alcohol-free, you may substitute with apple cider vinegar. This Swiss cheese fondue makes for a great start at a fondue party, especially when served together with crusty French bread slices and a couple of pickled vegetables. Let's start with this and the let the fondue fun begins.

Serving Size: 10
Preparation Time: 15 minutes
Ingredients:

- 8 ounces of Gruyere cheese, grated
- 8 ounces of Raclette cheese, grated
- 8 ounces of Emmental cheese, grated
- 1 ½ cups of dry white wine
- 2 tablespoons of lemon juice
- 2 tablespoons of cornstarch
- 1 garlic clove, halved crosswise
- Pinch of nutmeg
- Pinch of white pepper
- 1 piece of French bread loaf, cut into cubes
- 3 cups of assorted pickled vegetables

Directions:

- Heat wine in a pan on low. Gradually add the cheeses when the liquid starts to get bubbly, stirring continuously until completely melted.
- Combine lemon juice and cornstarch in a bowl until blended. Pour mixture onto fondue, stirring until smooth and bubbly. Season with nutmeg and pepper. Remove from heat.
- Rub garlic on the insides of your fondue pot. Discard the garlic.
- Pour cheese fondue on prepared pot, keeping the warmer on low. Place French bread cubes and assorted pickled vegetables in serving platters. Serve with the cheese fondue.

41. Truffle Fondue

If you love black truffles, this irresistible fondue will keep you dipping until the very last drop. This recipe features two great Italian melting cheeses—Fontina and Tallegio—that produce a velvety, decadent fondue.

Serving Size: 4
Preparation Time: 10 minutes
Ingredients:

- ¾ cup of dry white wine, plus more as needed
- 1 tablespoon of cornstarch
- 10 ounces of grated Fontina cheese
- 6 ounces of cubed Tallegio cheese
- 1 teaspoon of freshly squeezed lemon juice
- 2 tablespoons of black truffle tartufata mushroom purée

Directions:

- In a medium saucepan, whisk the wine and cornstarch together. Bring to a simmer over medium heat until thickened. Reduce the heat to very low.
- In a medium bowl, toss together the cheeses. Slowly add the cheeses to the saucepan and stir until the cheese melts and the fondue is smooth. Stir in the lemon juice and black truffle tartufata.
- Transfer to a fondue pot set to medium heat. If the fondue begins to thicken, add a splash of wine.

42. Fireball Fondue

This is a spicy and zest fondue that you can make whenever you and your guests are craving something on the spicy side.

Serving Size: 12

Preparation Time: 30 minutes

Ingredients:

- 1 ½ cup of cheddar cheese, grated
- 1 ½ cup of white cheddar cheese, grated
- 2 tablespoons of cornstarch
- 1 cup of lager
- 2 tablespoons of Fireball Whiskey
- 1 tablespoon of hot sauce
- Bread, cut into cubes and for dipping
- Vegetables, for dipping

Directions:

- In a saucepan over medium heat, add your Fireball Whiskey, hot sauce, and beer. Once your mixture has heated, reduce the heat and add both of your cheeses, cornstarch, and stir for about a minute.
- Serve your fondue with your favorite side dishes and bread.

43. Hawaiian Pork Fondue

This is a sweet tasting meat dish you can make whenever you need something both filling and on the sweet side.

Serving Size: 6

Preparation Time: 1 hour 15 minutes

Ingredients:

- 1, 14.5 ounce can of pineapple, crushed with juice
- ½ of an onion, minced
- ½ cup of honey
- ¼ cup of vinegar
- 1 tablespoon of soy sauce
- 3 cloves of garlic, minced
- 1 tablespoon of ginger, minced
- 1 teaspoon of coriander
- 1 teaspoon of cornstarch
- Dash of salt and black pepper
- 1 pound of pork tenderloin, cut into cubes
- Peanut oil, as needed

Directions:

- Pour the pineapple into a saucepan and add the onion, honey, vinegar, soy sauce, garlic, ginger, cornstarch, coriander, salt and black pepper.
- Stir the ingredients together well, then allow the liquid to come to a boil over medium heat. After boiling, reduce the heat and let simmer until the pineapple chunks are thoroughly cooked, approximately 20 minutes.
- Remove from heat and let the mixture cool for 10 minutes, then blend until it becomes a smooth sauce.
- Cut the pork into ½-inch cubes and add them to the saucepan, then simmer for 15 minutes.
- While the meat is cooking, add some peanut oil to a frying pan and turn the heat on to medium-high. The oil should begin to smoke slightly before you place the pork into the pan.

- Add the pork to the pan using tongs and cook each side for 3 minutes before moving onto the next side.
- Keep flipping the meat until it is fully cooked and browned, approximately 10-15 minutes. Once completed, remove the meat from the pan and place it on a paper towel lined plate.
- Stir the cooked pork into the pork fondue and serve immediately with grilled pineapple slices, fresh pineapple chunks, or a slab of French bread.

44. Cookies and Cream Fondue

If you are actually looking for a way to please those incredibly picky eaters in your household, then this is the perfect fondue dish for you to prepare.

Serving Size: 2
Preparation Time: 10 minutes
Ingredients:

- ¼ cup of butter, soft
- 1 cup of heavy whipping cream
- 24 ounces of white chocolate pieces
- 15 chocolate sandwich cookies, chopped

Directions:

- In a small saucepan over medium heat, combine the soft butter and cream. Stir constantly, until the butter has melted.
- Place the chopped cookies in a small pot. Add hot butter mixture to the pot and bring to a gentle boil. Boil for 5 minutes, until the mixture becomes a gooey consistency.
- Remove from the heat, and immediately add the chopped chocolate pieces. Stir until the chocolate has melted and the mixture becomes an even color.
  Allow to cool, and then place into fondue pot
  Pour with 2 inch of melted chocolate into fondue pot.
- Serve with your favorite dippers.

45. Luscious Caramel Fondue

With a combination of vanilla bean, cream, and sugar, this recipe develops a luscious tasty caramel that you can serve in varieties of parties and functions. Serve it with dippers, chocolate pound cakes, fresh fruit, or cookies.

Serving Size: 12
Preparation Time: 15 minutes
Ingredients:

- 1 split vanilla bean with the seeds scraped out
- ¼ cup of water
- 1 cup of heavy cream
- 2 cups of granulated sugar
- 1 cup of your favorite dipping ingredients

Directions:

- Pour all the ingredients into a saucepan, bring the mixture to a boil, until it turns golden.
- Remove from heat, let it cool and place it in your refrigerator for 36 hours (if you're a little impatient, you can use a moist towel to cover the caramel).
- After the caramel is chilled and ready to be served, place spoonfuls of the caramel in a small candy dish.
- Serve.

Conclusion

Fondues are so versatile. Actually, they can be anything from savory to sweet and something in between. But regardless what their flavor profile might be, it can't be denied that fondues are some of the best party superstars you must learn to make.

Don't worry. Concocting a fondue recipe will never make you sweat. It can be actually done in just a few minutes with just a handful of ingredients and without much fuss. What's more challenging is planning the dipping ingredients to serve around the fondue pot. It is much more of a bigger task than creating the fondue itself. So, make sure that you plan ahead and plan smartly. The key to hosting a successful fondue party lies in your ability to prepare the most suitable dipping ingredients, whether it's fruits or vegetables or bread or meats or a mixture of all. Be wise to mix and match, to bring in dipping ingredients that are in season and are easy to obtain, and of course, to make sure they taste lovely with your dipping sauce a.k.a. your fondue!

We hope you had a great time leafing through the vast collection of recipes in this cookbook as much as we did putting them together. These fondue recipes are luscious, tempting and outright delicious!

Happy cooking!

Printed in Great Britain
by Amazon

22090528R00051